MW00965984

THE GREATEST BUILDER FOR OUR LIFE

Richard Poulin

authorHOUSE®

AuthorHouse™
1663 Liberty Drive, Suite 200
Bloomington, IN 47403
www.authorhouse.com
Phone: 1-800-839-8640

First published by AuthorHouse 4/9/2009

ISBN: 978-1-4389-6645-8 (sc)

Printed in the United States of America
Bloomington, Indiana

This book is printed on acid-free paper.

Contents

Preface

During the course of our lives, we need to see the significance of how our lives on earth will determine our eternal destiny. As we establish fulfilling the purpose of our lives which God instructs us by living to worship Him (Isaiah 43:7), I would like to show you how to fulfill God's plan for you which is the way we can be most blessed not only for the present life, but life eternal. Almost everyone plans different agendas such as upcoming special events, trips with the family, financial planning, retirement planning and many other agendas concerning their present life here on earth. Even to the point of planning to the end of their lives should anything happen to them, leaving family members with death benefits. However, there seems very little planning on most peoples part concerning their eternal life. God instructs us in Colossians 3:1-3 that we need to set our affections on things above, not on things on this earth. This does not mean that we can't enjoy our life on earth, but we should not jeopardize our eternal goal by being so consumed with attaining goals that are so temporal, that we forget storing for ourselves treasures in heaven like the Lord instructs us because He is so interested that we gain greater valuable rewards that are going to last forever. When it comes to comparing our most temporal lives here on earth to the magnitude of eternity, it would make most sense that we should not jeopardize our eternal destiny simply for a moments glory and be stripped from everything we ever worked for. The book of Ecclesiastes identifies that unless we make Jesus the Lord of our lives and live by His plan and principles, nothing else is going to matter in the end. Even though one may attain all the wealth they can live the lifestyle of prosperity, work endlessly to raise a family and live till you are one hundred years old, without living according to the plan God instructs us to, our efforts are futile.

In this book, I would like to show you a wonderful plan God has shown me to be able to be established in the plan of God by living your lives with passion and purpose. When we initially have a plan to follow the One who created us, I also emphasize the importance that once we set our plans with God's purpose, we need to establish and maintain a relationship with God for our lives that fulfills His purpose. Finally, I will also identify what a person needs to do to preserve their lives in Christ, identify why it is that causes people to stumble by falling away from their faith and how to avoid ruining our relationship with God by remaining focused on His agenda for our lives and help you endure to the end by fulfilling His plan for you. In Jeremiah 29:11, the Lord tells us "For I know the plans I have for you, declares the Lord, plans to prosper you and not to harm you, plans to give you hope and a bright future". Because God has a plan for us, I would like to start off by seeing how valuable it is to have a plan with eternal rewards in mind.

Chapter 1

HAVING A PLAN

"For I know the plans I have for you, declares the Lord. Plans to prosper you and not to harm you, plans to give you hope and a bright future" (Jeremiah 29:11).

Like most people, we often tend to drift through life and just accept the things in life through different circumstances. Many people live through life with very little purpose and end up losing focus on what is important. Our lives are a terrible thing to waste. One of the greatest tragedies in life is a person who is about to see the end of their life, to look back and live in regret because he or she may have simply drifted through life with very little value or fulfilling no purpose and ultimately, failing to enjoy life which Christ says that He delights to offer us. In reality, each living soul should be valued as a priceless gift of God to every individual living on the face of this earth. Tragically, through many volatile activities taking place around the corner of the globe, it is hard to imagine that most of the world would put any priceless value of a human life like God Himself does. God's plan was to create man to fully inhabit the globe and worship Him and to live in His glory (Isa 43:7). When man failed to follow a simple command not to eat the apple from the tree of the knowledge of good and evil, God had a plan to redeem mankind through His Son Jesus because of the fall of man of what happened in the garden of Eden. God values us humans so much that He was willing to send His Son and live the life of many griefs, sorrows, being chastised by His own countrymen, being denied by some of His own family members and ultimately, being punished as He made His way to Calvary who willingly give up His life for us. God Himself was so focused with a plan for mankind in every arena in life, that He made it possible so we can enjoy every single facet of life each day to the extreme. With everything anyone could ever imagine, I don't think there is nothing else that could ever be created that would satisfy a human soul anymore than what is now created. Consider that millions of species of creatures, fowls, marine life, every type of terrain you can imagine along with the thousands of different shades of colour we enjoy seeing. Consider the millions of flowers, trees, plant-life to having countless electronics and comforts of life we tend to take for granted, while we fail to focus and enjoy what we take so much for granted. Sadly, too many people live through life being so busy and just simply exist without enjoying the journey. Many of these people fail to enjoy so much in life and forget what it means to truly live the way God intended for man to enjoy living. So what is a person to do in order to get focused and have a real perspective in his/her existence?

As you notice, the scripture at the beginning of this chapter in Jeremiah 29:11, God tells us that He has a plan for each of our lives, in order that we may have hope and a bright future. If God has spent the time to plan for each of us, we should also have a plan in place, otherwise, we fail to be established in hope and we forfeit our inheritance to have any bright future which He tells us that He longs to give us. It's up to us to accept His gracious offer of salvation and live according to the blessings of His word, or reject it. The choice is ours to make because God tells us in (Deuteronomy 30:19) that death and life, blessings and curses are before us, therefore, choose life! Christ admonishes us to choose life, but He gives us the responsibility to make that choice. When many people don't choose to live the life God offers us, we forfeit so much of our lives that is priceless, even beyond the entire worlds economy. God reminds us in Matt 16:26, what good is it to gain the whole world and lose your soul? God has given us a wonderful opportunity to enjoy every facet of life if we would choose to live according to His ways, which is His plan for us.

In order to have any hope or have a bright future, God had to first put a plan into place. Therefore, it is important that if we expect to have any hope or attaining a bright future for ourselves, we also need to have a plan in place. When you see houses, office towers or any man-made structures built, can anyone in their right mind think that these buildings were just built without having a plan or blueprints in place? Otherwise, any structure not having any plans in place during the building process will hardly expect to be structurally safe in the end. God reveals to each of us that He is far more interested in our lives than any building. He tells us in (Acts 11:26) that the children of God are in fact the church. He doesn't mention about a church being an erected building of bricks and mortar. When you read Matt 18:17, Jesus teaches His disciples to tell about His plan to build His church. In Acts 14:27, Paul mentions about the gathering of the church. It would be most unusual to think that buildings would gather together or consider speaking to a brick building with stained glass windows. Jesus mentions to His disciples in Matthew 16:18 about building

His church. So Christ Himself puts real emphasis to His disciples that He makes it His utmost desire to build His church, which are His people. He plainly says that He is most interested in us and delights to build our lives most effectively in order to live life to the fullest (read 3 John 2).

Therefore, when we see how important it is for God to have a plan in place, we need see how important it is for us to also have a plan. In order to have an effective plan in place, we need to have a goal in mind by which our lives are centered around God's perfect plan. In Prov 29:18 God tells us that where there is no vision, the people perish (NKJV). If you have a computer, go to the website at bible.com, and insert the word "vision", you will notice many times that God had revealed the word "visions" to many prophets in the Old Testament. When God wanted His prophets to speak to peoples of a nation, He often gave them visions so they can see the outcome of what will take place depending on the choices people make. He gave His prophets visions to warn the peoples of different nations of the devastating consequences of rejecting His commands which is ultimately centered around love. If you consider the ten commandments and the commandments in the New Testament, its all about living the life with His love which He tells us is what fulfills the law and the prophets (Matt 22:40). He also gave visions to His prophets to tell people of the blessings they would receive if they would choose to follow His loving plans. Chapter twenty-eight in Deuteronomy is one of many classic examples of the blessings of following Him or the curses of rejecting to follow His commands. Only the first fourteen verses talks about the many blessings in abundance that one could ever dream of, while the remaining chapter from verse 15 to the end at vs 68 gives us a graphic example of the extreme consequences for disobedience. When God warns us more often in greater length, it is like His cry to us and get our attention to refrain from living the life of disobedience because of the devastating consequences He so much wants to spare us from. His plan is beyond what we could ever comprehend or imagine. I would hate to think one day when I walk into heaven and happen to ask the Lord what is inside the big warehouse? And He should tell me that "this is the blessings I had for you, if you would have only chosen to live My way, but you would not!" Ultimately, when we visualize and focus on our existence in this present life, it is most wise to know how to live according to the plan God has for us during our time on earth, because it will determine our eternal destiny. When we live our lives on earth, it is also most wise to consider when we live according to the will of God, we are most blessed by living the blessed life, having inner joy and peace along with reaping eternal rewards.

Most people in life focus their goals, dreams and aspirations in this temporal world rather than the realm that will last beyond millions upon billions of years. The realm of eternity is beyond our comprehension, because this is the realm that has absolutely no end, and we forfeit our rewards and fail to store up treasures in heaven just to get a moments glory for ourselves here on earth, at which the expense of our very soul and having lost valuable rewards, is astronomical. God tells us even when we seek to receive praises from men, we have forsaken to receive the very rewards from God, whose rewards for us is incomparable to any rewards we could ever get on earth, because the rewards received from God lasts FOREVER. I capitalize this word to put significant emphasis on this because we don't have any idea the enormous blessings we forfeit by seeking to be instantly rewarded by others for a mere moment in time. This is very plain when Jesus instructs the Pharisees and the teachers of the law, that they will not be rewarded later, because they have already received their reward (Matt 6:1-4). God so much wants to bless us in a far greater realm than we can ever dream of. No wonder God admonishes us to set our affections on things above, not on things of this world (Col 3:2). He also says in 1 Cor 2:19 "No eye has seen, no ear has heard, no mind has conceived what God has prepared for those who love him." What a fascinating concept to think of the rich rewards that far exceed our human imagination, are reserved for us who truly love God as we delight to live by His precepts. The world has no idea what heaven is like. To most people, it's living on a bunch of clouds and watching a bunch of winged angels playing a harp, which seems to the deceived world that this would constitute as boredom. That is far from what the bible describes heaven. I highly suggest reading Revelation 21:10-27 before you go any further and just imagine the beauty of this kingdom. Our finite minds will never comprehend the beauty of heaven until those of us who have invited Christ into our lives and having our names written in the Lambs book of life (Rev 21:27b) will experience for ourselves. Just imagine walking the streets that are pure gold (not just "gold-plated" either)! Also, the seas being pure and clear like crystal and our eternal homes not being less than awesome mansions which Jesus tells us that no human hands could ever build. This is also a place described in the Bible where the flowers never fade, no darkness ever closes in because the glory of God shines its brilliance forever. Also, no sorrow, regret, sickness or tears are found in heaven. It's as though our past trials, sorrows, sins (which has been forgiven to us believers who repent) is never to be remembered. Only joy, peace, gladness and songs of praise fill the air in heaven. To me, this is far from what this world depicts heaven as, which is most unfortunate.

While the Bible describes heaven as far more beautiful than the human mind can comprehend, it also describes hell as far greater and far more horrible place of eternal damnation than any human could also comprehend. The most gruesome place of torture here on earth does not compare to the horrors of eternal hell which Jesus often describes. I often hear people say, why would God send anyone to hell? First, I want to inform you that God does not send anyone to hell, because He made a way through His Son to redeem us from sin, hell and the grave. For He wishes that none perish, but come to everlasting life (Matt 18:14). People who are destined for hell choose not to believe Him in what He says, which He often warns people the consequences of not following Him. That is why He tells us that those people are already condemned simply because they do not believe in Him (John 3:18). That priceless gift God had paid to send His Son to the cross to pay the penalty of sin on our behalf, the offer of what Heaven brings and the destruction of what hell is described should cause each person to want to do everything they can to be prepared to live in that awesome Kingdom of Heaven which only God could ever create. The description of how horrific hell is described in the Bible should also cause each person to do all they can to ever refrain from entering that eternal realm of destruction. If people do not agree that this message to describe hell should not be preached, why would Christ Himself talk more about the horrors of hell than He would talk about heaven? I truly believe He is concerned because He doesn't want any one individual to be destined to destruction. That is why He went to such extent in order to offer us eternal life, which He delights to give us in the first place. Unfortunately, anyone who has left this world denying Christ probably wishes this message would have in fact been preached more often. Just like the story of the rich man and Lazarus, where the rich man pleaded with Father Abraham at a distance to have Lazarus just even dip the tip of his finger in water just to cool the rich mans tongue because he was in agony and great torment (Read Luke 16:19-31). This horrible place is not just temporal, when some would preach as a temporal place of purgatory, but God Himself warns all too often that the consequences of denying the Lord and refusing to live according to His plan, is in fact eternal consequences with no hope in sight. If we could just grasp this truth, our gratitude and love for our Lord Jesus and what He has provided us to escape an eternal hopeless end to have an indescribable place of eternal glory, would escalate dramatically.

It's devastating to think that the rich man who cried in agony asked Abraham if he could send Lazarus to his fathers house and warn his own brothers. The sad thing about this is what he tells us that although people would rise from the pit of despair were to warn many people, they would still not believe (vs 31). The cost of not believing the love of God for us, His wonderful plan for us and His warnings to us is far more costly than anyone could ever imagine. I have heard before and I've said it many times, I'd rather believe in the Lord Jesus and live according to His ways, and be proven wrong than to deny Him and refuse to live His ways and be found in error to that! When we choose to live for Christ, we have nothing to lose, but when we choose not to live by God's plan and never accept Christs sacrifice for us, we have nothing to gain but so much to lose!

Our present life on earth is so temporal when we see and envision the boundless realm of eternity. To give you a segment of eternity, I will ask you to place two fingers about a centimeter apart, that would compare a life on earth of one hundred years compared and then looking up to either direction from one horizon to the other without ending, which is compared to eternity. Having this in mind gives us real perspective of the importance of how we see our goal and how to build our lives effectively in order to have an eternal value that surpasses what this world could ever offer. Our present lives here on earth is like a "dress rehearsal" in order to prepare our eternal home. The life we choose to live here on earth will determine our eternal destiny. But that doesn't stop there. We don't sacrifice living a blessed life here on earth to have the rich rewards of heaven. God wants us to enjoy life every single day! Just imagine for those who are parents, how much you want the very best for your child. God himself is able and willing to offer more for His children beyond what they could ever think or say (Ephesians 3:20). He tells us in Matthew 7:9-11 "Which of you fathers, if His son asks for bread, will give him a stone? Or if he asks for a fish, will give him a snake? If you then, though you are evil, know how to give good gifts to your children, how much more will your Father in heaven give good gifts to those who ask Him!"

When we value who God is and how much He loves us, He not only wants to richly bless us in an eternal kingdom, but also, to bless us richly while we are living this present life by living a life full of peace, joy, which no accumulation of money can compare. To think that we would forfeit an eternal inheritance just for a mere moment in our present existence to fulfill our selfish ambitions is a tragic reality for many. But many souls are living this way, and it doesn't have to be so. That is why God Himself gave us His awesome plan, which He tells us in His word, by sending His Son to shed His blood for us in order to redeem us from the curse, so that we can live the blessed life by building our lives most effectively in order that we may gain a rich eternal inheritance where no moth nor rust can destroy, nor thieves can ever rob (Read Matt 6:20,21). This means that our plan should line up with what God's plan is for us if we intend to live the most blessed life for this present life and eternal life.

If we want to reap the greatest rewards during our present lives and for eternity, we need to see the rich value of following God's plan for our lives. This starts by getting to know who God is. For some who may not have received Jesus to become their Lord, it all starts with the plan of salvation and asking Jesus, who died for our sins to ask and invite Him in our heart to be our Lord and Savior (read Rom 3:20; 10:9-10; Acts 16:31; John 3:16-18). The next step is to start developing a relationship with the Lord. This of course takes a lot of time, but God Himself knows this better than anyone. To learn to deeply love, build an enduring trust and expect to maintain a deep meaningful relationship with a certain person, you need to spend the time to get to know that particular individual. When I see my past as rebellious as I have been many times, I can't see who has been more patient with me than God Himself. If God is as patient as He has been with me all my life, I know that He is equally patient with anyone, because He went through much pain and agony, that we may have an opportunity to gain eternal life and not perish eternally as He often warns those who choose not to follow Him.

I will go over each step in detail in the next several chapters as we have this plan in place and our vision to store for ourselves treasures in heaven. It's important that we maintain our plan in order to follow God's plan for us and keep our sights on the goal that is heaven bound. Just like Paul admonishes us in (Philippians 3:13b – 14) "But one thing I do; Forgetting what is behind and straining toward what is ahead. I press on toward the goal to win the prize for which God has called me heavenward in Christ Jesus." So he himself identifies how important it is to keep our focus on the goal that will really count in the end.

When people fail to lose their focus on the goal which they have once set, their lives have often taken a turn for the worse and are being led astray. If you compare a ship leaving harbor to set sail across the Atlantic and it crosses through a storm, you can imagine that the ship would have easily been carried off course and would never make its destination if the crew on board had not kept their focus on the destination that lies ahead of them. So it is the same with our lives. The Lord Himself says that His people perish for a lack of vision (Proverbs 29:18). This is the ultimate goal, but there are many goals in life particularly important in order to follow what God would have us do. When we accomplish the works that God would have us do, this is largely part of our eternal rewards that we will inherit, because in the end, God will also reward us for our works (1 Cor 3:12,13). However, once we are saved, we are called to do good works, but we are not saved by our good works, lest anyone should boast (Eph 2:8,9).

When we want to determine what goal to have, we must see what our interests are and how we can best use them, which is what God has gifted us with. I always believe that when we inherit a particular interest in a certain field or work environment, this is what the perfect will of God is. When a person who loves the Lord, has a deep desire to go to a certain nation like Africa and help the poor, or pursue to help them as a medical staff, I believe this is God's will, because He has put that desire within your heart in the first place. He has intended for us to pursue and glorify God through what we desire. We are most effective at any given job that we desire to do the most. Therefore, in order for God's will to be done enthusiastically, wouldn't it make sense that He would use people who have a desire to accomplish a specific mission He calls certain people to do? As an example, I always loved math, which has now allowed me to become an Accountant, which I thoroughly enjoy doing. If I tried to be a mechanic or a construction worker, I would utterly fail, simply because I don't have much of an interest in those fields. God would not call us to do a particular task or go to a particular place if it is not our desire to do so in the first place. I couldn't glorify God with something I am not gifted at doing, because we are called to do all things for the glory of God (1 Cor 10:31). I couldn't imagine anyone who has a despondent look on their faces while they do any task, expect to be giving God any glory to the outsiders and onlookers!

Having a plan in place for our lives, means to have a goal in mind. When you read Luke 14:28-30, Jesus explains the importance to have a plan in place, which means that we need to set realistic goals and see how committed we really are. By not having a plan in place, we suffer ridicule from others saying: "this fellow began to build and was not able to finish" (Luke 14:30). When making a plan to fulfill our mandate in life, it takes time and effort because our very lives depend on it and we need to see the value by investing our time to fulfill our destiny. Individuals who do not use qualitative and quantitative time for setting plans and goals in their lives, tend to not put much value on their lives. We need to stop and think of how valuable our lives are here and now, because how we live our lives, will determine the amount of rewards we will inherit or suffer the perils and the level of destruction of our very existence in the eternal realm which has no end. I would advise you to let this concept fill your mind till it reaches your heart. The way to do this is to quietly and confidently meditate on this. In repentance and rest is your salvation, in quietness and trust is your strength (Isaiah 30:15). This concept is what identifies the wisdom of God who says "Knowledge comes easily to the discerning" (Prov 14:6b). This explains two theories. When we discern, or take the time to give thought to what God says, we will gain knowledge and understanding that allows us to live as wise men and women. The truth of God's word comes to those who will take the time to ponder and meditate of what He is telling us as we gain revelation knowledge and insight of the wisdom of His truth. In Daniel 2:2, God tells us that He gives wisdom to the wise and knowledge to the discerning. But, when we just drift in life, never giving any attention to what God is trying to tell us, we don't ever gain any knowledge and the truth of God's wisdom which is meant to build our lives most effectively. He tells us He is willing to give, but He wants us to come to Him because He is a God that is interested in developing a rich relationship with Him and with others (read 1 Corinthians 1:9).

After spending real quality time building your trust in the One whom we should, we need to determine what sparks our interest and have a vision to pursue a goal. Our goal we have in mind should be an end result of our pursuit. The next steps in the following chapters tells you how to build your lives most effectively by following an effective plan in place starting by laying a strong foundation, which Christ identifies as Himself (1 Corinthians 3:11).

Chapter 2

Knowing Where to Build

This is what the Sovereign Lord says: "See, I lay a stone in Zion, a tested stone, a precious cornerstone for a sure foundation; the one who trusts will never be dismayed" (Isaiah 28:16). "For no one can lay any foundation other than the one already laid which is Jesus Christ" (1 Corinthians 3:11).

In both of these passages, Jesus Himself is considered a foundation, which means that this is what we need to lay hold and be grounded in the knowledge of who He is, in order to effectively build our lives upon. If we want to build our lives in a way in order to live the most blessed life, we need to have a solid foundation. Every individual in this world has a foundation of some sort in their lives. However, not all foundations are safe, but are even destructive. Luke 6:46- 49, Jesus tells us what happens when we build our lives on certain ground. In verse 47 and 48, God tells about a wise person who hears His words and puts them into practice, is a wise person who digs deep and builds his life upon a rock. When the storms of life come, this wise person is established because he has come to put his trust in the One who is able to bless, provide, protect and preserve his life. The reason why storms of life come our way is threefold. First, we have an enemy, who is out to try to discourage us and keep our focus on our circumstances and ultimately, tries to destroy our lives by losing our focus of Jesus. Another reason why storms come our way is that when we use these storms and become relentless in our pursuit to trust God and rely on God, we become stronger in having a righteous character, and we are able to be stronger to help those who need help during their times of trials. It reminds me of a verse in Zechariah, where God says that we become secure when everything good is going our way, we have a tendency of becoming complacent, which God tells us that He is angry with a nation or people who feel secure which leads a nation to forget about Him (Zechariah 1:15). Thirdly, type of trials that come our way may in fact be beyond our control, but there are also times when storms and trouble come our way because we have forsaken the warnings that God gives us by choosing to do things our way, forgetting to acknowledge His help by making unwise choices. When God convicts us of our wrong choices, it is because He wants so much for us to get back on the path He has laid out for us. The devil simply accuses and condemns us to remain in feeling guilty which is like dragging a ball and chain.

Do you ever notice that when trials come to one of our family members, or a close friend, we learn to embrace one another and focus our attention on what is important by being there one for another, more-so than had nothing wrong ever occur. Just recently, one of my family members had concerns over some health issues. This actually brought our family closer by being in contact with each other more often, then had nothing ever occurred. It often makes me realize that our family tends to embrace and come together in times when someone is going through a trial, when we shouldn't have to wait for an unfortunate event to occur before it makes us realize the important issues we need to focus on. Trials in our lives are really a blessing when we trust in the One who truly loves us, which is the One we need to use as our foundation. Consequently, when you review the parable of the house being built, the other person who hears God's word, but doesn't put them into practice and gives no consideration for His instructions is like the one who built his house (his life) without a foundation, and became unstable when the storms of life came through. It even mentions that his life was completely destroyed (vs 49). I can't think of anything more graphic and practical than that. God never promises that we will not have storms of trials in our lives, but He does promise those who put their trust in Him, He will see them through.

Jesus is identified many times in the bible as the Rock (Deut32:4,31,37: Psalms 18:12; 28:1; 31:3; 62:2,6,7; 78:35). These are just a fraction of the scriptures that identify Jesus as our Rock. Many people who don't consider allowing Jesus to be Lord of their lives are basing their so-called foundation on some other principle. This other foundation, which is what many people trust most of all may be towards their job, stock-market, material wealth, stable retirement plans, monetary value. It may be believing in other false religions such as scientology, new age movement and other spiritual occultism such as the spiritists movement and many other false religions, which preaches false doctrine to identify that Jesus is not the Son of God, nor came in the flesh (2 John 7), or those who believe He did not ascend into heaven (1 Cor 15:17). Maybe it's simply trusting in themselves and their own ability to see and do things their own way. This is another faulty foundation! When Jesus is considered the Rock, this tells me that anything else is simply other than a rock, which means it is not stable. Putting and building our lives upon any other foundation other than Jesus will result in disastrous consequences, which He reminds us again in Luke 6:49. I can't stress how important it is to know where we must lay our foundation, and that place where we must build our lives upon a foundation is Jesus Himself. God Himself is love, and what this world needs is love. It reminds me of the song that people are looking for love in all the wrong places. The world is looking for love and needs love. What better foundation can we want to build upon other than the One who is perfect in love, power and wisdom, which is God Himself!! I can't think of any other foundation I would want to build my life upon other than knowing how much Jesus loves me and knowing how much He means to me. I am living proof of His love for me from the life I once dreaded and wanted to die, I am now living life to the fullest because I chose to live according to His plan for me. Knowing about the fact that someone should be willing to leave the comforts of His throne of Glory, and descend down to earth, to be born in the flesh, to experience pain, sorrow, suffering, be willing to shed His blood for me, I can't think of a better reason why I would not want to run to Him and gladly commit my life to His Lordship. I'd far rather love someone who would dare to do that for me, than to love "something" that doesn't or can't return any personal love or affection back to me. Whether we admit it or not, this is what everyone that has ever lived in the past, that is living presently or in the future, each one needs love and acceptance. That is why Jesus is able to satisfy the hungry soul that longs to be accepted. Sadly, much of the world would tell you that they don't want to have anything to do with religion when we talk about Christ. Believe it or not, I am not interested in religion either, because it's not about religion as the world would define as, but about having that wonderful relationship knowing Christ personally and what He means to me to restore and build my life with such hope and peace. Knowing about Christ and what He means to me, I can't think of a better foundation of which I want to build my life upon than Him.

Chapter 3

ESTABLISHING A STRONG FOUNDATION

Then he told them many things in parables, saying: "A farmer went out to sow his seed. (vs 4) As he was scattering the seed, some fell along the path, and the birds came and ate it up. (vs 5) Some fell on rocky places, where it did not have much soil. It sprang up quickly, because the soil was shallow (vs 6). But when the sun came up, the plants were scorched, and they withered because they had no root" (Matthew 13:3-6).

As we continue reading through chapters, I remind you to keep your focus on the goal and develop a plan which follows these biblical principles of how to effectively build your lives, which God often compares to building a house. When we are about to build our lives, we saw in the previous chapter how it is vitally important that we have a strong foundation, which is only when we make Christ Jesus our Lord. Even though we see that Christ is to be our foundation upon which we need to build our lives, the problem is never Christ, who is the foundation itself. But, often times, the problem is that we don't want to wait and take the time we need to invest in, to get to know Christ in such a deep personal way. Christ Himself is that solid foundation, so in order to have a strong foundation, we need to see an important principle of laying a strong foundation by spending quality time to get to know Him and what He should mean to each of us. One of the important principles we need to know in our hearts is that God loves us personally and is most interested in our well being. When we have come to establish this concept in our lives as absolute truth, this is what we need to establish in our hearts in order for our lives to be built upon the Rock, which is Christ. When we don't take the time to establish this truth in our hearts, we end up having a crack in the foundation and we attempt to build our lives without being as stable as we should be. Therefore, this foundation that we need to establish in our lives depends on how careful and how important we need to give attention to this. When you think of a foundation that needs to be strong, it needs to be immovable and be able to stand under great pressure. So when trials in life come our way, when we come to spend time to get to know the goodness of God in our lives, we won't become unstable and be crushed by the pressures this life brings our way. When many people will come to doubt the love of God in their lives when trouble comes, or even curse God, it is because they never took the time to get to know the truth about the love of God for them. This is what makes the difference when a person is stable in their relationship with God, and the other who is unstable, and bases their relationship on God depending on the circumstances they may be encountering.

When you read Jeremiah 51:26, God tells us this, "And O Babylon, they shall not take your cracked stones for a cornerstone, or any stone for foundations, but you shall be waste and desolate forever says the Lord". You will notice that when a nation or any person becomes desolate, it is because the foundation was not secure, by not relying and trusting in the Lord. Their foundation was made up of cracked stones by living for worldly ambitions without giving any regard for following the goodness of the true living God. This is what happens when we set our hopes on anything other than Christ Himself, our life becomes destructive and our lives remain unstable. In Psalm 11:3, the Lord indicates "When the foundations are being destroyed, what can the righteous do?" When the disciples asked Jesus "What must we do to do the works God requires?" Jesus answers them "the works of God is this: to believe in the One He has sent"(John 6:28,29). This tells us that it is more important to develop a right relationship with Christ, rather than focusing on our "works", or what we are supposed to do for the Lord. When we are called to do a specific service for God, those of us who have developed a rich relationship with him in the first place are able to do the works which God calls us to do.

Going back to the parable of the sower as mentioned earlier, the farmer sowing seeds describes what I want to emphasize the importance of taking time to grow in a deep fellowship and relationship with Him by really getting to know Him. Jesus Himself is considered the word (John 1:1,14) and the seed that He talks about in this parable is the word (the bible). When you pay attention to this parable in verses 4 and 5, it describes a type of plant that wants to grow too quickly without developing any roots. What happens to this plant indicates that it soon withers because it didn't take the time to develop roots, or develop a real relationship with the One whom we need to rely on. What is neat about each parable that Jesus tells His disciples, reveals a real message that applies to our present lives today as it did equally to them who lived two thousand years ago and throughout the ages. The principles of Christ's teachings is always valid for every human life, and is not limited to any timeframe in human existence. That is why it is absurd to believe that God's teachings were only meant for those who lived during the biblical era.

Much of the problem with us, who want to grow too fast is the result of thinking that we must "do" works to be justified. In other words, we think we need to receive God's approval because we accomplished many "good works." We tend to rush out to try to "do" rather then just sitting at the feet of Jesus and really getting to know about Him and His purposes for you in your life. Jesus gives us a principle when He talks about Mary and Martha. In (Luke 10:38-42), Mary comes to the feet of Jesus and listens to Him, while Martha is busy about many things. Jesus tells Martha that she is worried about many things, and what Mary chose is more commendable. Mary was interested in listening to Jesus and getting to know Him rather than trying to run around and being busy "doing," while Martha was more concerned with the cares and concerns of accomplishing tasks with a "to do" list.

This is encouraging for me personally, to know that it is good to just take time and decide to take a real interest to getting to know Jesus! This is what really pleases the Lord, because He wants a real deep relationship with us in the first place. When I was more concerned about rushing to "do" the works for God before I took the time to getting to know Him, I was often frustrated. I was trying to become a type of "Martha" rather than being the type of person that Mary was, which Jesus was more pleased with by just wanting to listen to what He had to say, spending the time with Him in the word and praying to Him, by just talking to Him and letting Him talk to our spirit. While we need to be busy and get tasks done, the important principle to reading about Mary and Martha is to put Christ first into our lives, and in particular, when we get an opportune moment, we need to spend that time with Jesus when just being busy doing things can sometimes wait.

When we see the importance not only to lay a foundation, we need to remain strong in the Lord which means we need a "strong" foundation. One of the main principles you need to develop by having a strong foundation include several principles such as:

1) knowing who you are in Christ (John 1:12);
2) know the magnitude of how much He loves you (John 3:16-18);
3) understanding God's plan of salvation for us (Romans 3:23; 10:9,10);
4) understanding that the very purpose of our existence is to live to worship Him (Isaiah 43:7) because we were made in the image of His glory;
5) knowing the truth of our dependency upon Him (John 15:5c);
6) seeing the importance of fulfilling the entire law of living the life of love for God and others (Matthew 22:37-40).

In the second principle, I purposely used the word "you" rather than us, because we need to take this personally for each of us. I want to emphasize that this takes time, but God Himself knows this better then we will ever! When a tiny tree is planted in a yard, a tree that is expected to grow tall needs to have deep roots dug into the ground in order to be strong. This is when it's important to be patient. Although we don't see results of a tiny tree or a seedling grow for quite some time, it is accomplishing a very important aspect, which is often hidden from our natural sight. Before you want to see life form of a tree from the ground, it is best to establish deep roots. This is of course most important because the tree or any plant that we expect to grow to maturity has to have established roots in order to benefit and sustain life at its best to receive its nourishment. Much of this understanding needs to be identified in our spiritual growth with Christ, if we expect to benefit the most out of our lives by really living for Him. Otherwise, when mighty wind storms come, I'd rather have this tree stand strong than fall down on top of the roof and perhaps destroying our house! Jesus often uses parables of using physical metaphors in order to teach us a spiritual principle which we must receive if we want to make the best of our lives.

One of the first important steps to getting to know God is to stop and meditate on everything you see around you and realize that He created everything before your eyes out of nothing and did so for the purpose that we may enjoy every facet of life which He created for our enjoyment. As part of a building process, I believe it's important first and foremost to learn about the sovereignty of God and learn about how awesome He really is. As an example, when you look at the starry hosts at night, He tells us that He has put every star in place, which in fact outnumbers the sands of the sea. To think that the stars in their greatness outnumbers the grains of sands, that in itself should be mind-boggling. I like looking at books that teach about astronomy, the galaxy, the Milky Way, the universe, it is a small glimpse of how awesome our God is, because He tells us that He fills all heavens and earth. When you consider the light traveling at a speed of 186,000 miles per second, and yet, it takes millions of years for the light to travel within a galaxy, it is beyond our imagination of the greatness of our God. Yet, God himself is so mindful of us! Some of the chapters in the bible I like to read concerning the awesome power of God is in Job chapters 38 – 41 (inclusive); Ps 91; 139, Genesis chapters 1 and 2 and Isaiah 45:18,19; 46:8-10. It's always interesting about studying more of the universe we live in, and makes me realize how little I know about the greatness of our God. When I hear about scientific studies and information they find out about the greatness of our universe, scientists have so far identified information from the Hubble scope in 1998, that they have sighted areas of the universe that they calculate is about 12 billion light years away. I'll let you do the math, but if you consider 12 billion light years; counting 12 billion is like counting 4 for every second without stopping if you were to count every second for almost a hundred years without stopping day and night 24 hours a day, 7 days a week. To also think that light itself travels 186,000 miles per second. I don't think we as humans can ever fathom the awesome size of our universe, which God Himself is that creator and designer of. Even the thought of scientific research identifies that there are approximately 80 billion galaxies in the universe is an awesome thought.

When you go back and read in Isaiah 45:18, God tells us that He created the Heavens (notice the plurality of heavens), and He fashioned the earth. When we think of the universe in its magnitude, and that we even exist in its enormity, we are told by Doctors and Scientists that there is a minimum of 41 factors in order to sustain life of a human being. Some of these factors include the position of the earth in a galaxy, the distance away from the sun, having the correct amount of gravitational pull, the exact tilt of the earth to allow changes of the seasons to occur, percentage of land mass to water, etc. With such details to sustain life, chances of us humans allowing to exist would be one percent of ten to the fifty-third power. That means you would have to start with a decimal and insert 52 zeros and insert the number one at the end, and having one percent of that ever occurring for humans to sustain life. Knowing this causes us to see how awesome our creator is, that He should even consider us. It's an awesome concept to think how much more faith it is to have the belief of being an evolutionist from knowing that we were wonderfully created by an awesome Creator like God. Just like the Apostle Paul mentions in Hebrews 2:6 "who is man that You O Lord should be mindful of him, the Son of Man that You care for him?" No wonder God is rightfully angry when we have no awe of Him, when you read the last part of verse 19 in Jeremiah chapter 2. I would far rather know that an awesome designer is the only One who could ever create us, being so fearfully and wonderfully made, than to think that we just happened to come into existence out of a blob of cells that just happened to form together by accident!!

When people don't believe they were fearfully and wonderfully created by an awesome designer such as God, I don't believe they value themselves as highly when only God Himself can ever create an anatomy such as a human being in every single detail to sustain life to the fullest. David Himself declares way back before Christ came to earth, of "how fearfully and wonderfully he was created by God" (read Psalm 139:14). This is really the start of developing a strong foundation, by being strong in the Lord and in the power of His might, by having that awe of Him in our heart. When we fail to develop the truth of having reverential fear of God in our hearts, we are simply being deceived from knowing the truth of the greatness of our God to begin with. That is why in Proverbs 1:7, He tells us that having the fear of the Lord is the beginning of having wisdom and knowledge. This fear of course is reverential fear. If it were based on any other type of fear, why would He want to draw us unto Him and have a loving relationship with us in the first place?

When we spend quality time to read and get to know the reality of the awesome attributes of God, we can learn to establish our trust in the One whom we know is all powerful. The same thing holds true, that when we see how God knows each one of us personally, knows the numbers of hairs on our heads, keeps His eyes of protection upon us, and see how mindful we are in His sight, we come to know the reality that He does love us so much. This means we can enjoy that wonderful relationship with the One who is able to provide for our needs, protect us from all harm, sustains our lives each moment as we take each breath and has prepared a way to enjoy everlasting life of endless hope, joy and peace because we come to know the truth about how much He truly loves us and is able to care for us. This is what we need to study on what we read in these chapters and just meditate on these wonderful truths until such time as it gets into our heart. This is where roots start to develop. When we take more time to read His word, which is His love letter to us, our roots begin to grow further down and dig deeper down. So when we do face trials, we know whom we love and put our trust in Him to help us no matter what. I like what it says in Romans 1:16 "I am not ashamed of the gospel, because it is the power of God for the salvation of everyone who believes: first for the Jew, then for the Gentile." In 2 Tim 1:12, "That is why I am suffering as I am. Yet I am not ashamed, because I know whom I have believed, and am convinced that he is able to guard what I have entrusted to him for that day." So, when Paul did suffer much, he was not moved or deceived, because he developed such a deep relationship with God by trusting Him no matter what, because he knew that he knew that God loved him, no matter what. This is what made him such a great Apostle. He had developed such a loving and trusting relationship with God that him and Silas together sang in the prison cells and gave praise to God regardless of the present dark situation that faced them (Acts 16:24,25).

Another great verse in Jeremiah 1:5, is when Jeremiah himself acknowledges the awesome foreknowledge of God, that He should know him before he would ever be formed in the womb. This awesome wisdom of God, who is able to create us and fashion us to enjoy every aspect of life, should cause us to reverently put our entire trust in the One who has this infinite wisdom, knowing in our hearts that He knows best. By spending quality time and reflecting on these wonderful promises, you can appreciate the awesome knowledge of this truth about God. As you may see, when a person does not take the time to reflect on this truth about Him, we miss out on so much and have been robbed by the one who wants to keep us blind from having a deeper relationship with God, which is satan.

Therefore, when we need to see where to lay our foundation and to build our lives most effectively and positively, we need to look to the One who created all things, who loves us because He died for us, who wants a loving relationship and longs to give us eternal life that is extraordinary, which He alone is the only one who can offer us that. Jesus tells us that "no eye has seen, nor ear has heard, no mind has conceived what God has prepared to those who love Him" (1 Corinthians 2:9). Lets look to the One that loves us and wants to give us the gift of the fullness of life and life eternal is such a deeper way, that we will not want to live any moment from living the blessed life when we delight ourselves to be held in His loving hands. No other source, religion, spiritual dimension or any person offers what Jesus has accomplished for us and is able and willing to offer us.

In order for us to build our lives upon Jesus (who is our solid Rock), we need to take our time and get to know who Jesus really is in order to establish our lives on firm ground. This does not mean we take 10 minutes and pretend that we know Him, or just spend a meager one hour session in church once a week. But it is imperative that we really take time to consider how awesome He really is and how we need to value our lives before Him in a deeper and most profound way. Feeding our spirit by getting to know Him through the word is just as prudent as the requirement of feeding our physical bodies. Living by His instructions is like medicine. We can't expect to be spiritually healthy if we aren't feeding our spirit with the goodness of His word. Just think if you only ate once a week, we would be so physically weak, we would hardly be able to do anything. So when people spend about that much time in one week or even spend less time than that to give our attention to God, we can't expect to be strong in the Lord either.

In order to truly love someone intimately, you need to know deeply about that individual. You can't expect to say you truly and deeply love someone if you don't spend real quality time to get to really know them in a deeper way. Therefore, the first thing that I find is very important is when we want to have a solid foundation, we need to take the time to get to know about who Jesus is and how important He really is for us to have any value in our lives. When we gain an understanding of who Jesus is and how much He loves us, we are laying our lives upon a solid foundation that is based on the truth of how dependable we need to be to Him as our very life. Jesus tells us that He is the way, the truth and the life and no one can come to the Father but by Him (John 14:6). Building our lives upon any other doctrine or philosophy is simply building our lives on a false hope, which means that we will end up being deceived by believing on an agenda that does not give us any hope, but a hopeless end. It is important to note that we take the time to keep and maintain our focus to understand who Christ is how much He does love us, because so many people who have initially given their heart and lives to Christ have ended up wandering away from Him because they lost their focus to follow Him and have easily forgotten His love for each of us. Other times when people turn away from God, they end up replacing Christ, by setting their Pastor, or some other human leader as their example. The leaders they once looked up to, failed them at one point or another. When this happens, people tend to become upset and fall away because they did not have their focus set on following Christ in the first place. It is Christ that we need to build upon and keep our focus on following His example. This is a clear example of what happens when we don't know where to lay our foundation and what we should be building our lives upon does not last when we fail to focus where to lay our foundation of our lives in order to effectively build upon. Although we need to see our Pastors, Elders and Deacons as the church leaders, we have to be careful not to put them on a pedestal that we loose focus on whom we are to be focused on in the first place, which is Jesus.

Over the years, I have admired a teacher of the Bible whom has since passed away sometime in the mid to late 1980s. This teacher, whom I got to know and admire from reading and listening to his material is Hobart Freeman. I remember about 18 years ago, hearing him mention something that has stuck with me to this date, which I very much appreciate. He said to the congregation, that when he simply taught the word to them, he would tell them "don't just believe me because I said it, check it out in the Bible for yourself!" Also, he mentioned at the same time; "that if I Hobart Freeman ran and jumped off a 10,000 foot cliff, does that mean you are all going to do the same?" I cannot respect anyone more than having that kind of humble attitude, that he would purposely instruct people not to put him on a pedestal, but to focus their attention on the One who died on the Cross for them and is the redeemer of our salvation by being our sacrifice and shedding His blood for us.

When we learn to lay our foundation on a principle of what we believe, we need to ask ourselves "what do I believe and we should answer our own question to ourselves about why we believe what we believe in." This is why it is so important that God's word is the final authority to what we base our belief on. This is establishing that strong foundation on which we are able to build our lives safely and effectively upon.

Chapter 4

Building Up Our Lives

"Except the Lord builds the house, they labour in vain who built it, unless the Lord keeps the city, the watchman wakes, but in vain" (Psalm 127:1).

At the start, we need to continue to have a vision as to what type of "house" or, in other words, what type of life we would want to see the Lord help us build? If most of you wanted to compare your quality of life compared to a house, you would most likely choose a grand looking mansion, rather than a decrepit and unused building that is about to be condemned. Our type of life compared to many different mansions is quite different from anyone else's. Some may have ambitions in opening up a business, doing research, full time ministry, health care or mechanics of some sort. For some, it may be caring for the elderly or for others, it may be working in the mission field home or abroad. Just because a person isn't in to full time ministry, doesn't mean it's not God's will for you. What would happen if everyone wanted to wanted to be a Pastor or Evangelist, and we had no mechanic around to help fix your car? We need to see what sparks our interest and determine what we are talented in. Whatever vocation or hobby we set out to do, the main important thing we need to remember to do is doing all for the glory of God (read 1 Corinthians 10:31).

In Hebrews 11:10, we see that the Apostle Paul was talking about Abraham who was looking forward to a city with foundations, whose builder and architect was God. In our lives, God is more interested in building our lives by allowing Him to be our builder and architect. So our question is: How do we allow God to be our Builder in the first place? When a person continues to understand the knowledge of who God is and we continue to learn how to build our relationship with a loving and awesome God, we become delighted to allow Him to be our "builder and architect" of our lives in the first place. By allowing the One who created the universe, the earth and all its inhabitants, we need to understand that the Bible describes who God is and the exact expression of His love towards us. When I hear scholars saying to others not to take the Bible literally, I don't know what they are basing their theory upon! An example of what I can see when we are not to take the Bible literally is when Christ says that He is the vine and we are the branches. Obviously, this is speaking figuratively and not literally. But it has a profound message of who we are and how much we need to depend on Him who sustains us in the first place.

We need to see the Bible as our "lifeline" for our soul, just like food and water is to our bodies to keep us alive. 2 Tim 3:15,16 tells us, "How from infancy you have known the holy scriptures, which are able to make you wise for salvation through faith in Christ Jesus. All Scripture is God-breathed and is useful for teaching, rebuking, correcting and training in righteousness, so that the man of God may be thoroughly equipped for every good work." The reason why I mention this is because even a lot of Ministers and scholars only use many of the scriptures as a guideline for their own agenda, not realizing that the entire scriptures written are God's instructions for us, if we expect Him to be the Builder of our lives. Otherwise, we end up becoming our own builder, which will end up being full of flaws, if we fail to allow God to build our lives according to His perfect plan. His word is His perfect plan and will for our lives. Again, it is important to note what He tells us in Psalm 127:1, "Unless the Lord builds the house, its builders labor in vain. Unless the Lord watches over the city, the watchmen stand guard in vain."

That's why I strongly emphasize to initially study the sovereignty of God and His greatness and really meditate on these scriptures that tell us how great He is (Job chapters 40 – 42; Psalm 139; Jeremiah 1:5). When I came to understand the God I serve as an awesome God from studying some of these scriptures, I come to the point that I would not want anyone else, or any other belief system try to build my life other than God Himself. When we understand that Jesus is the word right from the beginning, which was later manifested in the flesh (John 1:1, 14), we will see our need for living according to His word which will be what we need to build our lives upon if we expect to receive the very best for our lives not only in the present, but for all eternity. When we are most effective by allowing God to build up our lives, it is because we come to love His word and delight to seek His counsel in how to live, because we first know the truth of how much He loves us and wants to give us the very best by following His counsel. We will no longer follow Him out of duty, but out of love, which is what He intended for us to live in the first place.

In order to fulfill His plan and allow Him to build us up, we need to know what the greatest commandment for us to fulfill is. In Matt 22:36,37, a teacher of the Law asked Jesus, Which is the greatest commandment in the Law? Jesus replied: "Love the Lord your God with all your heart and with all your soul and with all your mind. This is the first and greatest commandment. And the second is like it: "love your neighbor as yourself." All the law and the Prophets hang on these two commandments. Because God is Love, our ambitions in life and all we do in life has to be the result of our love for God and for one another. Otherwise, its like the verse indicates in Psalm127:1, we end up laboring in vain by trying to accomplish our dreams and goals in life that will bring us no eternal rewards nor have any eternal value. God tells us that when we labor for God, the works we do is not in vain and we don't give up (read Gal 6:9). What a tragic loss of remorse and regret when we see how we have held little value or regard by refusing to follow His ways simply because we wanted to follow our own agenda and seeking our own ambitions without having any regard for Christ.

When I want to get the most out of my life, I have come to understand and know from my experience, that I inhabit peace that surpasses all understanding, I have gladness in my heart and have that immeasurable joy within when I delight myself by following God and follow His loving ways. This is priceless, because all the money and the richness of this materialistic world we long for does not satisfy like having a rich relationship with our Lord. It's something I may not understand fully, but I can say truthfully, that knowing what I now know from life's experiences, that there is nothing more satisfying than knowing you are following the One who loves you and was willing to die the shameful death on the Cross for you. Like the Scriptures itself indicate, that there are very few who scarcely would die for a friend, let alone die for all the world, including the rebellious, like I once was. Knowing that He is so merciful and gracious to me now, He chooses to pardon me of my sinful ways and the best thing is when I repent, He chooses to forget them, as though I had never sinned.

After we establish the truth about how much He loves us deep down in our spirit, we are able to allow Him to build our lives effectively as our Builder. One of the most effective ways we allow Him to build our lives is to come to the knowledge of His word and get the most of His word for us. The way we do this is to realize that His word is our very life-line and the key to receiving the greatest eternal rewards, having far greater eternal value than simply not following His instructions or simply by following another philosophy. In John 6, Jesus had many disciples, which were His followers. After He had mentioned about Himself being the "Bread of Life" and how He mentioned about those who wished to follow Him must eat of this "Bread", many of His Disciples had decided to leave Him. This is one of the several indications that people who are followers of Christ, may one day decide to turn away from Him. Being a Disciple means to be a true follower of Christ. Many disciples who were followers of Jesus did in fact end up turning away from Him. Many people who do not believe that a follower of Christ would ever lose their salvation would often say that these disciples were never His followers in the first place. If it were so, they would not have had the title of being a disciple. You cannot be identified as a disciple if you're not a follower of Christ in the first place. The Bible explicitly identifies those specific group of people who decided to leave Him and His teachings, were considered His disciples beforehand (John 6:66). Jesus turned around and then asked the remaining twelve disciples (as we know of them), if they were going to leave Him as well. I like Peter's response in vs 68, "Lord, to whom shall we go? You have the words of eternal life. We believe and know that you are the Holy One of God." Peter knew the value of who Jesus is and the eternal value His word has.

When we see the value of His word, we will be able to become truly knowledgeable gaining such wisdom and understanding, which the world, who chooses not to follow Christ cannot ever comprehend. One of the fascinating concepts I realized most recently is when I came across a scripture in Proverbs 14:6, where it mentions that "knowledge comes easily to the discerning". When we want to come to the knowledge of Him, the value and the wisdom of His word, we need to spend time meditating and giving thought to valuing Him as our "life". You will also notice that He is able to impart this knowledge simply because we choose to take the time to give thought to His ways, not because of our intellectual abilities. In 1 Corinthians 20-31, God tells us that He shames the wise and prudent by choosing the humble and abased (vs27). No matter how smart or how simple someone happens to be, true knowledge of knowing Him and the wisdom of His word comes to those who will spend quality time to getting to know Him. There is nothing like having the knowledge and wisdom of His word to get through each day by living with such immeasurable joy, gladness of heart while living in total peace from all fears. Today, fears of many circumstances grip so many people because they have failed to know about Jesus, of what He has done and what He can do for us. Those who end up living in fear are the ones who have put their trust in commodities, governments, economy and other types of material resources other than relying on the Creator of the universe and establishing a rich relationship with Him. Most recently is a classic example of how the world is in fear and turmoil because of the global economic crisis going on. Knowing the truth of having a right relationship with God gives us peace when we know how He is able to provide for our needs. This is one of many great reasons why I love the Lord because we are never at the mercy of any circumstances that God is not able to take care of us. When fear grips the world, those of us who come to love and trust in God, will continue to live in peace while many people become a victim of fear that faces much of the world.

In the Sermon on the Mount, Christ instructs those who are listening. In Matthew 5:6, He tells us that "blessed are those who hunger and thirst for righteousness, for they shall be filled." This means that Christ Himself is our righteousness, and when we have a desire to come to know Him, He fills us with the richness of having knowledge, wisdom, understanding, joy unspeakable and such inner peace, that no amount of money can ever compare to it. Having knowledge of His word is what sets us free (John 8:32,33), otherwise, we end up living in a false sense of hope and a false sense of security. By having gained knowledge of Christ, who is the Way, the Truth and the Life (John 14:6), this is why we can have such inner peace. Therefore, the first thing about building your lives, in order to have eternal values, is to understand the value of who Christ is, the value of His word because He is considered the word who became flesh (John 1:1,14).

Next, when we want to have our lives built up in the richness of His blessings, we need to see how important prayer was in the life of Christ. If He, being the begotten Son of God needed to go to pray often, how much more do we need to go to Him in prayer? Most times, many people think you need to kneel down on the floor in order to pray. But, most importantly, its simply pouring your heart out to Him, confessing your need of Him to help you in every area of your life and being in conversation with Him. This allows you to open yourself up to Him to be honest with yourself and simply talking to Him about what is on your heart and then to be still and listen to how He instructs each of us. When you have spent the time to develop a relationship with Him in the beginning, you can get the most out of prayer, by believing that He is more than able and willing to help you in your time of need. When people don't spend the time to getting to know about Him, they may often pray in vain, because they don't have the assurance that God hears them and delights to answer prayer (1 John 5:14,15), or they are uncertain if it may be His will to answer prayer. Jesus tells us in James 1:6-8, that when a person is unstable when praying by questioning or doubting that He will ever answer our prayer, they fail to receive anything from the Lord. Therefore, the Lord is not pleased when we doubt His love, protection and provision for us.

Another very good reason to getting to know much about Christ, is that we develop a stronger faith and that hope that does not fail. The reason I say this is because there are a lot of Christians that don't believe it is God's will that we be healed. I have talked to several Christians who tell me that they don't believe in the "health and wealth" gospel! No wonder God tells us in Ephesians 3:20, that He is willing to do much more for us than what we could ever ask or think. Also, this prophetic word of God is proof that the devil does in fact rob so many Christians (John 10:10a). When I meditated on God's word about healing, I came to the conclusion and asked, "if it is not God's will to heal, why would He have mentioned so many times about Him healing people?" Also, if it weren't His will to heal, why would He have willingly suffered by being whip-lashed so many times? Otherwise, He would have done this all for nothing. In 1 Peter 2:24, God tells us that "we are healed by Jesus stripes." In other words, when people don't take the time to study the word itself, and they simply take the words from someone else and don't bother studying, it is sad to see how much people miss out of the blessings of God if they would spend the time in prayer, read by studying the Bible, and seeking what His will is. No wonder the devil is able to rob many people from being blessed. This is why, when many people are not strong in the Lord, it is because they don't care to spend the time to study His word. Again, if a lot of people spend the time to eat food as they do spending time with God, it won't be too long before their bodies give out entirely. The devil may not rob some people, who have received Christ's invitation of salvation, but he is able to rob them of the many blessings simply because they don't take the time to know more about Jesus and what His will is for us. When I found out about how many people are being robbed just because they listen and receive the wrong message, I always check to see what God has to say about a matter. This is why it is wonderful to seek knowledge of God's word. Especially, when it comes to doctrine like healing. I would far rather live my life in divine health then being in sickness and just accepting it. I am more assured that it is His will that we be healed, because in 3 John 2, He explicitly tells us that it is His will that we prosper in all things, and walk in divine health, just as our soul prospers. I don't know about you, but I far rather accept His teaching than listen to any other teaching! This is why it is so true that having the knowledge and wisdom of His word far exceeds all the pure gold and silver one could ever attain in this world. His word tells us it is life to our soul and health to our bones. When people often bring discouragement of what they say, I often find that God says something totally different, which encourages my soul. I realize what He tells us that His yoke is easy and His burden is light. It's like choosing to be blessed when we cast our cares upon Him instead of carrying our burdens from our past that weigh us down. But that is what many people choose without real-izing it, because they choose other than what God Himself clearly tells us by simply listening to others without com-paring it in the light of what Christ Himself says. When we come to another beautiful concept of the knowledge of His word, we see how important it is when we speak in line with His word. In (Proverbs 18:20, 21) God shows us how important it is that what we speak, has the power to bring healing to our body and soul, or bring destruction. It's no wonder, I cannot emphasize enough about living in the blessedness of having this knowledge. As living proof of this, when I continually speak health to my body and bones, I can't even remember the last time I was ever off work due to sickness. I realize more and more, the blessings of getting to know Him by reading His word as I delight to pick up the Bible and expect to be blessed from this. This is the beauty of having and gaining knowledge of the Bible.

It's choosing life over death, which God gives each of us a choice to make (Deuteronomy 30:19).

One of the effective ways I find by gaining knowledge of reading the bible, I often read audibly to myself. Psalm 91 is a classic example and one of my favorite chapters. When I quietly read this passage, I give thought to what He is saying to the general population, then I read it audibly and insert my name as though He is speaking to me personally. This allows me to hear as though God is speaking to me because He is interested in each of us personally. When I read this again, the words are so comforting that I shed tears of being so grateful to God and knowing how much He loves each one of us. This also builds my faith, which pleases the Lord (Hebrews 11:6) because, in Romans 10:17, it tells us that faith comes by hearing, and hearing the word of God. So in order for us to hear the word, we need to hear it audibly. To me, this is very important that we speak His word and personalize it. As an example, when you very well know that a loved one, whom you know loves you, it is special to actually hear that person speak those words to you. It's not simply enough just to know they love you, but it makes it extra special to hear those words spoken.

Earlier this year, a young child had accidentally died from an event that was supposed to be a fun event, turned out to be a tragedy. I knew this family, and of course, I felt saddened. When I began to speak about this unfortunate event to my supervisor at work, as soon as the words came forth from my mouth, it was then that I broke down in tears. Even through this unfortunate occurrence, I realized something interesting at that particular time. The words spoken at that time caused an increase of compassion within myself had I not spoken a word and just kept it within, which caused me to weep for the first time regarding this incident. Similarly, when we speak His word into our lives, we see the genuineness of His love for us in a far greater capacity than if we were to silently read His word. This holds especially true when we read and speak His word when we come across passages like "O how I have loved you with an everlasting love" (Jeremiah 31:3). This is special when you speak this and insert your name as though God is speaking directly to you.

One of the other main reasons why God can't be a builder in many people's lives, is that many people question God and remain bitter and forsake Him because of the tragedies that occur in this life. The reason why they do is because they have failed to see Him as the One who is able and willing to be the Builder and Restorer of our lives. Many people focus on the adversities of their lives and become bitter from their negative experience. If these same people could see how God is able to show His love in order to build and restore lives, they would become better rather than bitter. I can easily say that from all the unfavorable circumstances I endured, I could have become bitter, which would not have done myself any justice, or I can rely on the One whom I learned to trust and lean on, and realize how awesome He is, who was able to turn my life around and restore my life to live to the fullest. We allow God to be a most effective builder when we simply learn to trust in Him because we first learned the important step of how much He loves us. Most people who remain bitter towards God have never bothered to read the Bible and read how God intended for us to live. They end up justifying their emotions which are leading them to become bitter, which ends up destroying so many lives. That is why so many people are being destroyed, because of the lack of knowledge of the truth about His love for us and His willingness and ability to heal, mend, restore and build our lives to the fullest. In John 10:10, He tells us that He has come so He can give us life in abundance. This life in abundance doesn't just refer to money, but it emphasizes the entire realm of ones life, which includes being rich in health, relationships, knowledge, wisdom, spiritual richness of having the peace of God within, living life by having that joy within no matter what circumstances may be happening around you, and finally, enjoying life not only in the present, but for all eternity. This richness also includes the fact that if a person has gone through adversity, they are the ones who are able to comfort those who are going through similar unfavorable circumstances. The result is building rich relationships by reaching out to one another. God cannot show His love of restoration if we never had to be restored in the first place. You cannot have mountaintops in your life if you don't have valleys either. Just imagine how boring life would be if everything was always on an even plain. We would never appreciate the good times if we never had to go through unfavorable times in our lives. It reminds me to think how fickle the Isrealites could be after being enslaved in Egypt for around 430 years, to start grumbling against God and against Moses only 3 days after their freedom from bondage. This is a humble reminder of how I see myself when I start to murmur when I should have been thankful if I had kept focused on how many times God has truly blessed me. These are the areas that God wants to help build our lives by seeing the positive aspects of life, in which we personally, physically and spiritually benefit from.

I like what God says in (1 Corinthians 2:9) "No eye has seen, nor ear has heard of what God has prepared for those who love Him." Love can never be forced, nor does He force His ways upon us. He wants us to draw unto Him, and He promises that when we do, He will never leave us nor forsake us. Christ Himself mentioned that he could not perform miracles in His own hometown, because of their unbelief (Matthew 13:58). God admonishes for us to choose Him, which is how we exercise love. If God were to force His ways unto us, this would mean that man has no freedom of choice, and our relationship with him would be more robotic than a genuine heart relationship. He encourages us and describes Himself awaiting for people to reach up to Him as He continually reaches down to us, just like He mentions in the old testament when the nation of Israel continued to turn away from Him (Read 2 Chronicles 30:7-9). Often, it is when people are down in the gutters that they learn to cry out to God and reach up for Him. At that moment in time, it is then when people realize that the Mercy and Grace of God is there to pick them up, heal their past, restore their present and build their future with everlasting hope, peace and joy. So when people remain bitter towards God because of unfortunate events, these negative circumstances turn out to be a blessing when we realize that God is truly merciful and has His outstretched arms reaching down to pick us up and be that effective Builder of our lives when we are submissive to His good and perfect will.

The devil's plan is to keep us focused on our circumstances, which is most unstable because one minute, we can be standing on top of our circumstances and then suddenly, it can come to a sudden crash. Christ Himself wants so much for us to be strong and stable by keeping our focus on Him and His love for us. He Himself has proven His love for us by willingly suffered greatly in all magnitude physically, emotionally and spiritually. We should also then go through a fraction of the pain and suffering He did for us, so we would prove our love for Him. When we do, it is rewarding when we remain strong in the Lord because we have built our foundation knowing He loves us regardless. It's unfortunate that much of the world would say to a Christian, you are weak. I would dare say it is entirely the exact opposite of that. When a person who denies Christ and has their hope set on anything else, they are the ones who end up worrying and becoming fearful. When others have set their hope on Christ, and have developed that loving relationship with Him, they are the ones who are able to remain strong through the storms of life. I don't know about you, but I'd rather have His peace within me of keeping me strong in the One who loves me than being lead by fear. This is just one of the reasons why you cannot put a price on what it is like to have a wonderful relationship with Christ and coming to the knowledge of His word.

When people don't want to allow Christ to be the Builder of their lives, they think that by following Christ, they will have to give up on so much of life. I like what one of my respected teachers of the word, Joyce Meyer often says, when a person has to give up on things to follow Christ, what they will have to give up is harboring bitterness, anger, bondages, worrying, fretting, storing up unforgiveness, hatred, envy, jealousy, being stoned or having a hangover the morning after, or similar traits. When it all comes down to it, these are really the only things we give up when we follow Christ. I can't understand why anyone wouldn't want to give up on these attributes that do nothing but not only ruin ourselves but also negatively affect everyone in our life whom we are close to. But the problem is that most people don't see the freedom of really living for Christ. People who choose not to follow Christ, they remain blind to the bondages they continue to live in when they choose to go their own way. Living in sin blinds many people from the consequences of their sins and blinds them from the freedom they could be living by following the Lord instead. Jesus tells us that when we have come to know the truth (Jesus), this is what sets us free (John 8:32). I can't imagine why anyone in their right mind would not want to be set free? This is what it means to experience true joy that we have when we see the blessings of following Him and seeing the wonderful plan He has for us.

I have really experienced the fact that when I used to see my ambitions of having lots of money, working hard just to acquire an abundance of material possessions, I realize now that I was in real bondage back then. Had I remained in that type of lifestyle, I would have looked back on my life and realized that I worked hard just to accumulate things in life without ever really enjoying life, which is a sad reality for a lot of people. But living that lifestyle and choosing to remain living in that lifestyle, I didn't see myself in bondage until such time that God Himself had to put me through severe trials in order to release me from remaining in bondage to covetousness. Even in my early years as a Christian, I realized I was in bondage to a covetous lifestyle. The reason why I now know I was in bondage was because I was never satisfied until such time that I fulfilled the dreams I once had of living the "good life." Now, my ambitions are so different than they were 20 years ago. it is a blessing to know that I long to live to bless the less fortunate with my giving, especially for the people I have met who live in the country I have recently visited in Zambia.

Before I became a Christian, I would have thought that having this type of ambition in life would have been living a dull and lifeless existence. I can now truly say that it is a real blessing to let the Lord, who knows best, and truly loves me, be the true builder and architect of my life. I can look back on my life now, had I been so determined to go my own way in life, I can tell you that my life would have taken a turn for the worse. Even apart from the trials I have gone through, I can truly say that God had His mighty hand upon me and I can truly say that I am much better off knowing that He lovingly directed my life to be used mightily by Him. Had I not gone through the trials of suffering greatly from my past, I know for sure God would not have been able to use me to help others in similar needs during their time and suffering. I can't tell you how grateful I am for God to use someone like myself to have stopped a precious life from committing suicide. I never realized this until I was down and going through a valley of circumstances. When a lady replied back to my email while I was asking for help, she told me that I should read some of my replies when I counseled her. She told me that others and myself who had responded to her email had stopped her from successfully committing suicide. This continues to remind me that when someone loves the Lord and wants to live to give Him glory, and live to be a blessing to others, there is no limit to what God can do through simple people like myself to fulfill His purpose. Although He could do it all Himself, He would rather use us to fulfill His purposes and plan in order that He may have something to reward us. God desires to reward those who are obedient to Him. He tells us in Hebrews 11:6b that He is the Rewarder for those who diligently seek Him. He also tells us that He greatly rewards those who even offer a cup of cold water to those in His name (Matt 10:42). We serve a God who loves to reward people, because He wants so much to use us in order to reward us for our obedience to Him. This is one of the primary focus we need to remind ourselves about storing up treasures in heaven, of which these treasures He talks about is His way of richly rewarding us for all eternity. In Matthew 6:19-20, God encourages us to store for ourselves treasures in heaven and not on earth. In other words, we need to live to do the works of God in order to be rewarded for all eternity than to just focus on accumulating things on earth that we think will satisfy us, which only does for a very brief time in our existence compared to eternity.

When we come to know our Lord in a very deep and personal way, we realize how awesome He really is to us and how He continually preserves our lives, protects and provides every aspect to sustain our lives to the fullest. This is allowing the Lord, who is our greatest Architect to build our lives to live with purpose.

Chapter 5

Establishing Our Lives

"So then, just as you received Christ Jesus as Lord, continue to live in Him, rooted and built up in Him, strengthened in the faith as you were taught and overflowing with thankfulness" (Colossians 2:6,7).

One of the important steps we need to maintain is establishing what we know about our relationship with the Creator. Many times, you will hear about many people who once loved the Lord and desired to follow Him, no longer seem to be interested in following His loving ways. God warns us that there will be many people falling away in the latter days giving heed to seducing spirits (1 Tim 4:1). To contemplate falling away, that means a person would have had to have faith in a loving relationship with God in the first place. For God to indicate that someone has fallen away, the sinner who has never received Christ in the first place can never suggest they will fall away, when they were always fallen and never raised with Christ in the first place. Many people will quote the word and say that God promises never to leave us, nor forsake us (Heb 13:5). This proves that God is so faithful and merciful to us, but the other side of the coin we need to remember that we as humans, who are fallible may be the ones to leave Jesus and forsake Him. One of Jesus own disciples, namely Judas Iscariot, who would have had to be a follower of Christ to be considered a disciple ended up betraying Christ Himself and then went off to commit suicide. Jesus tells us that it was better for Him not to have been born then to betray the Son of Man. He even remarked to one of the disciples that "one of you is a devil." I can't imagine Jesus telling someone that and remained saved without repenting. A fellow preacher who I have heard was alongside Billy Graham in his earlier years of preaching the message. This same person had later left the ministry and had later denied Christ altogether. Years ago, when I was looking around the bookstore, I was curious to read what was written in a published book titled "Farewell to God." This particular author was someone who once accepted Jesus to be their Lord and personal Savior, and to my horror, has now indicated in this text that denounces Christ and tells people to forsake God. I have also personally met a friend who once loved the Lord and had the radiance of Christ whenever he spoke of Him, at which time, he now does not want to have anything to do with Him. This is the purpose of why we need more than ever to be established in our relationship with Jesus. Peter tells us in 2 Peter 1:10, to be all the more eager to make your calling and election sure. Although we are saved by His Grace, God still gives us the responsibility to press forward and continue to develop a deeper relationship with Him. The Apostle Paul tells us the he presses on to meet the higher calling which we are called heavenward. Therefore, the Apostle Paul identifies about pursing and persevering to do the work God has called him to do. What I have found helpful that motivates me is to meditate on His great love for me from the agonizing suffering He went through for me personally. When I see the quality of my relationship with Christ is in relation to others, I am motivated to want to be a blessing to others simply because I love Him, because He Himself first loved me. When I am motivated by His love, I have seen extraordinary works accomplished because He gives me the strength to do it in the first place. It's when I step out that I find His grace is sufficient. The point of the matter is that we need to step out and let God do His wonderful work through us. I find I receive less of His strength when I feel lazy and find myself wasting most of the day doing very little. The story of Peter stepping out into the water is a good indication of how we are to step out if we are to be of value when we focus on Christ to give us strength in the first place.

Christians who have fallen away by no longer following God has taken their focus off of Christ and what He greatly and willingly suffered in order to redeem someone so unworthy such as I. Earlier in this session, when we come to know the reality of the exceeding love that God has for us, why would we ever dare to turn our backs on Him? When all along, He paid such a great penalty for our sins to such an extent, that He willingly lived as a humble servant, wearing no royal robes, never walking in a home with marble floors or luxury bedrooms. He chose to live humbly as a servant, was willing to wash His Saints feet, when we should have done otherwise. He was acquainted with much sorrow, was often chastised just so that we could have peace. He bore the punishing blows that causes bruises on the flesh just so He would pay for our iniquities. He bore those horrible painful whiplashes and chose to receive these lashings in order that we can be healed of every sickness and disease. He was the least deserving, and yet He willingly accepted these marks of brutal punishment, just so we as human beings who deserve such punishment could be set free. I often think of the songs that remind me of how grateful I am that God Himself should willingly take the penalty on my behalf. Songs like…"He paid debt He did not owe, I owed a debt I could not pay" and also "Lest I forget Gethsemene, lest I forget thine agony, lest I forget thy love for me, lead me to Calvary." When we focus the truth of His love for us in such a profound way, we will be able to be steadfast of being loyal and true to the One who willingly went to such extreme extent to be so mindful of us to offer us such a glorious hope of eternal life. This is what it really means to establish our lives, just like a house that is solidly built is established when renovations and improvements take place in the house. The trouble, turmoil and trials that may come our way, will not be able to shake us because we have established our lives by fixing our mind on that solid Rock that the bible identifies Jesus as.

This is that awesome peace that He is able to offer us, which no one else, or nothing else is ever able to offer. When we establish our love relationship with God, He is able to offer us hope. When we deny His offer to have a wonderful relationship with Him and don't allow Him to be the builder for our lives, deep down inside, people have very little hope of securing deep peace within. The world would be happy when favorable circumstances would come their way, but sadness soon fills their face when troubles come. They are bound by their circumstances, when otherwise, the person who knows the Love of God for themselves is able to have peace within that only He offers, no matter what the circumstances may bring. Anyone in their right mind should rather choose having hope and peace than despair and restlessness. The price Jesus paid for us goes beyond our comprehension, because it is not natural for any of us to believe that someone, even our closest family member, relative or friend should dare do as much as Christ Himself willingly did for the sinner, which in most terms, means that the sinner is the one who is rebellious and a mocker. Not only that, but Jesus offers us so much more than the world is able to offer, because no amount of money could ever compare to the richness of having peace, hope, wisdom, knowledge, joy unspeakable and full of glory, having divine health and prospering in every arena in life. Sadly, even Christians do not accept the wonderful offer that Jesus gives.

I have heard many Christians tell me that they do not accept the "health and wealth" gospel. I have mentioned to one who admitted that he was sick, and I wanted him to say the prayer of God's promise to heal (1 Peter 2:24; Exod 15:26; Psalm 103:2-4). There are so many scriptures telling of what Christ offers just in healing alone by paying the penalty while bearing so much pain. I often think that it is more painful for Christ for so many people, especially Christians, to deny His offer which He suffered, just because we don't feel worthy or to simply choose not to believe that this promise is for us today, just as much as it was for those who lived in the Biblical era. When Paul was talking about having a thorn in his flesh, he was talking about having to deal with people, not sickness. When someone denied my kind offer to buy a coffee for him and he went and then bought his own coffee, it troubled me that he would not accept a kind offer. If this minor incident troubled me enough to just mention this, can you imagine the magnitude of such gift Christ offers us, how He must feel when He graciously offers us a life of overflowing blessings for free, and we deny His priceless offer? Yet, so many people forsake the greatest gift of salvation and His gracious offer of prospering in living in divine health as one of the many gifts He offers. This is what happens when people are not established, because they lack in the knowledge of the truth of how much He loves us, how much He suffered for us, the abundant life He longs to offer us (John 10:10b), also prospering in every area of our lives (3 John 2). He reminds us in Hosea 6:4, "My people are destroyed for lack of knowledge" simply because we reject knowledge of His love, grace and mercy to us. A lot of people, and sadly, many Christians fail to receive these wonderful promises of living the prosperous life because many of those people fail to appropriate His promises that He wants to offer. No wonder Paul says in Ephesians 3:20 "God is willing and able to do exceedingly and abundantly more than what we could ever ask or think". This tells me that we have limited the Grace and Mercy of God so much in our lives that we have allowed the enemy of our souls to rob us, of which he is fulfilling his wicked and devious plan (John 10:10a). Before we can expect to live the prosperous life in every detail, we need to mature in our walk with God. Otherwise, blessing a covetous person with additional finances is like giving a sharp knife to a three year old. Therefore, what is meant to be a financial blessing to this type of person will end up doing them more harm than good.

When we want to live an established life and get the most of the abundant life He offers us, we need to go back and remember to set our focus on Jesus. Focus on developing a relationship with Him by getting to know Him and how much He loves us and values us. We need to understand more by humbly receiving His Grace and Mercy with thanksgiving and determine to stop ever thinking we don't deserve His offer. If we ever deserved anything good from God, then His Grace and Mercy would mean nothing. That is why His Grace and Mercy is considered His "gift" which is why we could never deserve it or earn it. This wonderful gift is immeasurable because when we do receive the goodness of His favor, it is only because of His Grace and Mercy to begin with. We need to learn to accept His offer and receive it.

Another very important principle we need to come to know, is that we also have to understand how to appropriate His promises and use the principles of His Word. For example, when people will talk negatively about themselves or continue to speak about themselves being sick all the time, they don't realize that they are playing into the tricks of the enemy. For God is trying to teach us to use our words wisely and speak His Word to heal us. Proverbs 18: 20-21 tells us "from the fruit of our mouth, a mans stomach is filled, with the harvest from his lips, he is satisfied. The tongue has the power of life and death, and those who love it will eat its fruit." Therefore, if we expect to have victory over sickness, we need to heed what God says, use His instructions and start declaring what He promises. Again, many don't experience this because they just accept whatever circumstances come their way, rather than fighting the good fight of faith and coming out on top. I can truly say that in over 28 years I have been employed, I remember only ever having to take half a day off being sick, other than being seasick which I was on the ship in rough seas. I have learned to appropriate His Word, which is His promise to us and pray healing scriptures over myself continually. That is why we need to speak His word over us. I just finished watching Dr. Phil earlier this evening and a young girl who is about

26 yrs old continues to be tormented after 13 years earlier of experiencing verbal and sexual abuse that she went through which lasted around 3 months. This is how devastating negative words have over our lives, because what is spoken to us and about us enough times, builds a stronghold in our spirit and we end up believing the lies of the enemy who tries to condemn us. That is why we need to understand the power and the authority of God's Word over us and start to declare the wonderful precious promises of His Word over us. We need to speak His Word over us and believe what He says about us to get into our heart. This word we speak from the Bible, is the same spoken word that Jesus used to defeat the enemy. This is why, when Christians who don't know any better, they don't appropriate this awesome truth and they often live a life under satan's lies and deceptive ways that rob the fullness of life Jesus offers. In Revelation 12:11, satan is identified as having deceived the world. So that means, at this moment, he continues to deceive so many when it doesn't have to be the case.

I can't thank God enough for the wonderful truth of knowing His Word. Had I not known about this wonderful promise, I could have easily continued to live a despairing life like I once felt like several decades ago. When I am often confronted with accusations and negative words spoken against me, I simply go to God's word and speak the wonderful and powerful promises over myself. Just like a powerful scripture found in Isaiah 54:17 "No weapons formed against you will prevail, and you will refute every tongue that accuses you. This is the heritage of the servants of the Lord, and this is their vindication from Me declares the Lord." I can tell you truthfully as the Lord is my witness, that speaking the power of His word with the authority in which He gives us (Luke 10:18-20) gives me victory over being defeated by developing low self-esteem from negative words being spoken. I choose to believe what the truth of the Bible says over anything else that would oppose His encouraging word. This is another wonderful revelation of the power of knowing Christ and what it means to walk in victory (Rom 8:37). When I use scriptures in brackets, I would ask you to audibly declare them over you. I also remember a time where a supervisor would tell me that I would not ever be able to accomplish a certain goal. As soon as he said this, I felt saddened and beginning to feel hopeless. I soon got fired up in my spirit and outright told the devil (not my former boss mind you), that he is a liar and I verbally declared the promise of God in Philippians 4:13 For it is written: "I can do all things through Christ who strengthens me." As soon as I spoke that word, I felt such surging power of God's Spirit upon me and the invisible walls of which was built up, came to a sudden crash. I have never experienced such power like that. The point to remember is that I could have been defeated had I not appropriated His promise by declaring and speaking His Word over me. That is why it is so important to know His word which is able to establish us and make the difference between living the life of defeat by believing the lies, or living in victory by knowing the wonderful truth and promises of His Word.

Another fallacy that the world has been deceived about Christianity and having a wonderful loving relationship with our Lord, is that they feel that being a Christian is boring. Actually, I have been on both sides of this issue, and I can tell you in all truth that it is far more exciting being a Christian than not being a follower of Christ. For one thing, Christianity is anything but stained glass, pipe organs, somber type music and sermons that hardly keep your eyes open. I have been to the best worship service in the middle of the country where a church building had nothing but bamboo poles with no walls and a thatched roof in southern Zambia out in the middle of the country. The people would be singing, shouting and clapping hands singing and praising God because they simply had developed a personal encounter with Him. When people fellowship with others who truly love the Lord by following His plan and allowing Him to be the Builder of their lives, they have the greatest fellowship and enjoy an uncompromised hospitality. Also, people who not only just received Christ to be their Lord, but invite Him to build and enrich their lives by being submissive to Him, are the ones that stand by your side when you are being faced with trouble, they go out of their way to pray for you, help you in any way they can and truly go out of their way, leaving their own agenda to be there to help you in any way they can. This is what the plan of Jesus is for our lives when we follow His example. It's exciting that the One who created the universe is the One who enables us to fulfill the greatest mandate of any human existence. If you would just simply consider, there is no greater reward because you desired to do a good deed for someone else and determined to be a blessing to someone in need. When you bless someone else, rewards are multiplied in many ways. People who receive whatever good deeds you do are blessed with kindness and peace, you are blessed with joy unspeakable and know that God will also reward your good deeds for all eternity. When we let God build our lives, I like to think that He is not only a

God who adds, but He goes on further to identify that He is a God who multiplies.

When I meet mature Christians for the first time, in a very short time, I feel as though I've known them for a lifetime. If Jesus would not be the centre of our lives, we would never have known one another and would be living alone, not knowing what a wonderful relationship we can experience with one another. When people share a common denominator with Jesus as our Lord, we share a common bond that is life changing and life enhancing that brings hope from despair, beauty from ashes, and the oil of joy instead of mourning (Isa 61:3). Joy fills their empty hearts that is only known to those who have ever received Christ.

The friends who have made such a positive impact on my life were the ones who live following the loving examples of Jesus. There is absolutely no comparison when you befriend someone who loves the Lord. I can truly tell you that when I compare to the many wonderful friends I now have because we share a wonderful relationship with Jesus, I would far rather have these friends whom I can rely on and trust than hanging around with people in my younger years who I thought were often my friends, turned out to be anything but. Especially when there are times you need to find someone to console or trust. Sharing the same values by developing a wonderful relationship with Jesus allows us to be strengthened in times of storms which makes the difference of looking forward to another day by being encouraged, or facing are tomorrows with despair and loneliness. I have been in both of those realms and knowing Christ as the center of our lives is what really makes the difference.

By following the plans of which Christ who is able to effectively build our lives, He gives us peace that surpasses all understanding when others who reject Him try to fill that emptiness unsuccessfully. He liberates us from bondages that we feel we need to do to keep us happy, such as heavy drinking, smoking, going to hard rock parties, swearing and typically living a rebellious life. We will notice that when people who rely on circumstances that eventually went sour, instead of setting their trust in the Lord, fear, unrest and every negative effects start to eat away at them.

When we read the instructions of His wisdom and knowledge, He provides the absolute best medicine for our souls. The Book of Proverbs is truly a book of wisdom and insight that literally and physically brings health, healing and wholeness to our whole being. For example, where He tells us that envy is like rottenness to the bones (Proverbs 14:30), it does just that. It eats away and destroys the health to so many people. Many of those who oppose God and blame God for sickness that devastates life, don't realize that He tells us how we can live a healthy life if we would just take heed and follow His example. When you forsake the One who loves you personally, you cannot expect to live in victory when you shut out the One who pleads to help you. It is sad that those who oppose God and blame God outright deny His instructions, end up bearing negative consequences.

Christ Himself was the most selfless person who ever lived, whom displayed the radiance of God the Father. I have seen time and time again, that those who live selfishly and cater to themselves without giving any thought to the benefit of others have a countenance that is anything but peaceful and carrying a bitter spirit within themselves. Thousands of those whom I have come in contact and have come to know, who are so giving and generous are the ones whose radiance bears the glory of Christ. God in His awesome knowledge tells us in Ecclesiastes 8:1b that "wisdom brightens a mans countenance." The reason why there are some who portray Christs radiance is because they are filled with His peace simply by obeying Him because they understand His love for them. When there are those who rebel against God, or those who delight to follow His loving ways, I notice that each one of them fulfill His prophetic word of what takes place when we choose to follow Him or not. From my previous lifestyle of living a rebellious life, to now following His loving ways, is a result of living each day with a glorious purpose, living with hope, living with inner peace that I have not encountered until I invited Jesus into my life as Lord of my life. I cannot emphasize of what it means to let the greatest builder of our time, be able to restore our life, build our life and enhance our life to live each day with Hope and purpose. I can say this with a clear conscience because there were times before that I just wanted to die because I was more fearful of living than I was of dying. I felt I had no hope and was of no value to society. I even commented to my own mother one day when she mentioned to me about a school teacher who lived right across the road from us, and his brother got electrocuted while working on a grain elevator in western Saskatchewan. I immediately commented to her "why could that not have happened to me instead?" I can't imagine how devastating that comment must have been to her. This is what it means, now that I have come to personally know Jesus. When I asked Him to be Lord of my life and asked Him to rule supremely in my life, I received such hope and peace that words cannot express how wonderful it is to know someone who could love me so much that He suffered and died for me, while I was yet a sinner living rebelliously several decades ago.

When I reflect on my life and what Jesus has done, this is why I cannot say enough of what God is able to build, establish and restore our lives. This is why it is so important for Christians to remember what Jesus has done for us so we don't fall away, like the Bible says, many will do in the latter days (1 Tim 4:1). Finally, to establish our lives effectively, we need to refrain from having a childish attitude and play the "blame game" with each other. Unless people stop pointing fingers and blaming others for their situation, these people will never grow up in the Lord and mature, which God so much wants for us. Can you imagine a 25 year old acting like a young child? God warns us in Isa 58:9, that as long as we point the finger and accuse, we will not receive His blessings which we so desperately need if we expect to be established in our relationship with Him. This also suggests when people have a critical attitude towards one another. The problem with having this attitude is that these people forget that it is only by Gods Grace and Mercy that we are not living the rebellious life we could be living. This is one of the bigger issues that cause Christians to fall away from a wonderful relationship they once had with God and with others. I cannot emphasize how important it is for everyone to benefit by taking steps to grow in the Lord and be established by having a right relationship with our Creator while having a right relationship with others.

CHAPTER 6

PRESERVING OUR HOUSE

In this chapter, you will notice that it is particularly longer than the other previous chapters, but this is an indication that in order to endure, we need to consider many areas of our lives that may creep in and destroy our relationship with the One in whom we have first established. To continue on from the last chapter, we need to understand why it is that many Christians left their first love with God in the first place in order that we may guard ourselves from this occurring in our lives. That is why the Bible warns us that our enemy goes around like a lion seeking whom he can devour. We are more strengthened to preserve our well being when we learn to apply the principles of God's Word and desire to gain knowledge, wisdom and understanding of His word to us. We are also more strengthened to allow God to preserve our relationship with Him when we identify areas that cause many to stumble and be able to refrain from giving in to these temptations that our spiritual enemy would have us cave into. This chapter will help identify areas people are prone to backslide and identify how we can avoid this. I find what helps is when we come beyond just knowing His word, and really come to a real deep understanding of the wisdom of His word to us. It's one thing to just know, but additionally to understand because God tells us in Proverbs 4:7, that we are encouraged to get understanding. Jesus identifies the importance to gain understanding in addition to our knowledge of His word. I would like to emphasize how important it is to come to understanding a concept rather than just knowing about any issue that we may have to deal with, whether favorable or not. In addition to what He is saying, He emphasizes a vital importance. He says that even if we have to sell everything to gain understanding, we need to do that if we want to have the best for our lives. In other words, we need to put His agenda in one of our high priorities if we expect to get the most out of living a purposeful life, which He intended for us to live. As an example of gaining understanding in addition to having knowledge, let us look at an example of what Christ tells us about forgiving someone. As we know, God instructs us to forgive those who have trespassed against us, so that we also will be forgiven by God. As we know, the natural man will know what this means, but will lack the understanding of why and how, we see that we can often fail at this attempt to forgive when we don't understand why we need to appropriate this. The person who lacks understanding will often justify their feelings that violate the instructions of God, even though God Himself is quite clear about forgiving. This concept is what it means to simply have knowledge on its own. When we apply understanding to this scenario, we will identify that our oppressors who may come against us are simply victims of the real enemy behind the scenes, who is the devil and his angels. For God tells us that we do not fight flesh and blood, but principalities, powers and rulers over darkness in high places (Ephesians 6:12). When our oppressors are more vulnerable to be used by our spiritual enemy, the devil can use these people even more-so to come against God's people. That is why Jesus warns us that our greatest enemies may be those of our own household (Matthew 10:36), because the devil knows who to use and who he can effectively use, which are often the ones whom we are close to. When we understand the entire concept of seeing our oppressors as a victim of the enemy instead of ourselves being a victim of the oppressor, we will be stronger to fulfill what God instructs us to do by having compassion and mercy towards others. We don't end up being a victim of circumstances by harboring bitterness and unforgiveness, which only ruins ourselves. But, we will have more compassion on those who do come against us because we will see their need and have concern for them rather than focusing on ourselves, and entertaining a "woe is me" attitude and that self-pity spirit that ends up eating away at us. This is one of the vital attributes and an awesome concept to see that having knowledge is not enough in itself. As you just read from one example, applying understanding makes a remarkable difference to be able to either stand firm, or crumble within. This is why Jesus was able to say to His Father, "forgive them for they know not what they do", when He was being crucified. Stephen was another Godly man mentioned in Acts where he himself was being stoned, he also asked God to forgive them. What a powerful testimony. This is a classic example of a person who has to have an extraordinary strength of character. This is what makes certain Christians strong whereas others going through similar situations would simply crumble within because they lack wisdom, knowledge and understanding of living according to God's principles. There are certain Christians who fall away simply because they lack understanding in order to effectively apply the truth of God's word in a deeper way.

Like anything we own, if we expect any resources we have in our possession to last, we need to take care of it to preserve its lasting quality. Especially, when we own vehicles, the longevity will increase dramatically if care is given to it. As we compare any products we buy to keep it in good shape, we can expect the same thing when it comes to preserving our soul and our relationship with the Lord. Although salvation comes at a moment in time when we receive and invite Jesus to be our Lord (Rom 10:9,10), sanctification, like developing and preserving our relationship with God and with others is a life-long process whereby we need to continue to preserve our very soul. For God tells us that he, who endures to the very end shall be saved (Matthew 10:22). Preserving our soul is like sanctification, it becomes a lifelong commitment and gradual growth. In this chapter, I want to identify with you some of the areas where people who once had a wonderful relationship with God, suddenly have backslidden and no longer enjoy the fullness of life that comes from having a healthy relationship with God. We need to identify some of the areas which caused many to stumble and fall away, we need to identify and consider why this is happening in order to keep this from happening to us. It's like comparing the comforts of a house that has been filled with beautiful furnishings and then the owner returning home after thieves came in and destroyed, to find the house empty and bare.

Anyone who is a homeowner, continually needs to upgrade his home, make renovations, continual maintenance upkeep to clean and care, and other minor repairs that crop up. Many unfortunate incidents by natural disasters have devastated homes. As horrible as it has affected many people's lives, these buildings can often be replaced. Christ

Himself puts emphasis on His interest more-so on our lives, because, as homes can be replaced, it cannot compare to our spiritual, physical and mental well-being of a human soul, which means that a human soul cannot come with a price tag! No material in this world will ever compare to the vitality and sacredness of a human soul. Christ Himself emphasizes when He says in (Mark 8:36) "what good does it do to gain the whole world, yet lose your soul"? Therefore, no matter how much riches one may acquire, it will never compare to the value of a human life. This was also emphasized when He told a parable about being the Pearl of Great Price. This was identifying that His sacrifice for the sake of human souls far exceeds the entire world's economy. When we identify the value of a human soul and the extent of what Christ allowed Himself to go through for our sakes, this is the beginning of understanding of the care we need to take in order to preserve our very soul and the souls of others we come in contact with each day. Therefore, as the average homeowner makes arduous attempts to maintain the preservation of homes, cars and other tangible material items, we need to consider more-so to preserve our relationship with our precious Lord Jesus and with others.

When we neglect taking care of our homes by not keeping it clean, doing required minor repairs and cosmetic upkeep when times of wear and tear shows its age, it won't be long that mold spores will appear and leaky pipes that appear to be minor may prove to be disastrous if neglected. It is the same when we don't take care of our entire well being. The qualities of a Christ-like character may give way to careless life of sin and rebellious behavior, which Christ compares to as serious as witchcraft. Unfortunately, many men I know will be mindful to look after their vehicles with the utmost care by hiding every scratch, polishing away every fingerprint and smudge, while at the same time, these people deteriorate inwardly by not taking care of their own bodies by unhealthy eating habits, lack of exercise and not guarding their heart and mind to stay positive with the instructions of His word. When you read Luke 11:24-26 Christ says "When an evil spirit comes out of a man, it goes through arid places, seeking rest and does not find it. Then is says, I will return to the house I left. When it arrives, it finds the house swept clean and put in order. Then it goes and takes seven other spirits more wicked than itself, and they go in and live there, and the final condition of that man is worse than the first." In other words, when we have been pardoned but just remain idle and don't fill our minds with God's goodness and don't invite His Spirit to help guide us each day, our empty vessels get filled with destructive thoughts and ambitions which ends up destroying what we have allowed God to build us up until now. This is why when we need to preserve what we have established our lives upon Jesus, it takes work and perseverance on our part. God tells us to persevere in James 1:12, "Blessed is the man who perseveres under trial, because when he has stood the test, he will receive the crown of life that God has promised to those who love Him."

One of the segments that allow the greatest architecture to build our lives is to confess our dependency upon Him. In today's society, we are being ingrained to be "strong" and "proud." The two are not always bad to a certain extent, but when becoming proud turns out to become arrogant and turns our gratitude away from God to say "see what I have accomplished," a great devastation awaits these people. In one of the greatest books that I call "the book of wisdom",

God tells us that "Pride comes before destruction (Proverbs 16:18)". Therefore, the fact that pride may or may not come before destruction is not the issue, it is the fact that it will definitely come, regardless. I must admit that I have experienced this truth and proven this theory to be correct more than I care to admit. This is what happened to satan, who was once called Lucifer, who was considered one of the high arch angels that was highly adorned with precious jewels and was given much wisdom. But when he became filled with pride, this was the start of his destruction when God stripped him of his high position and hurled him to earth (Isaiah 14:4b-20). This ugly pride that entered into his heart was because he looked at himself as having more beauty and wisdom that all the other angels, as though by his own power, he alone had attained it. Pride is a spirit that fills many people's hearts today because they come to believe that they have made great accomplishments on their own strength and wisdom, and have forgotten the truth of their ability being a gift of God that was given to them in the first place. This is why people are blind to the truth, because no one in their right mind can ever justify pride in the first place. Jesus tells us in (1 Cor 1:27-31) that He shames the wise and prudent by choosing the foolish ones so no one can ever be truthful and boast within himself (read vs 29). I have witnessed many times, when people would become proud and tell others of how many people they have lead to the Lord, as though they did it by themselves, they would be the first to fall away from God. God reminds us that it is His Spirit that draws people unto Him in the first place (John 6:44). This also reminds us in Matt 26:31-35, when Jesus told His Disciples about how He was to face death. Just after Jesus tells Peter that He would deny Him before the cock crowed, Peter would proudly say that even if he had to die with Him, he would not disown Him. Of course, we know soon after that Peter outright denied Him, Just as Jesus predicted. Reading these scriptures is a reminder of how fallible we are and how vulnerable we are when we become proud. Again, these are the same people who no longer have a wonderful relationship with Christ they once had. Allowing ourselves to become proud allows the enemy access into our lives, which is why God tells us that He opposes the proud, but gives His grace to the humble.

In similar circumstances, God tells us in Daniel chapter 4:28-37, about King Nebuchadnezzar who ruled Babylon, was walking on the rooftop and exclaimed about how he built this kingdom. Soon after he had spoken this, he was humiliated to the point that God stripped him of his high position to live amongst the wild animals and ate grass just like cattle. It wasn't until later that he confessed, when his sanity returned to him, of his powerlessness and how God is in fact the One who appoints people to positions and is the One who gives gifts and abilities. Another thing to point out is that when he became humble and sanity was returned to him, this is also an indication of how pride blinds our minds, our knowledge and understanding of the truth of our dependency upon God. We need to remember that these different stories we read in the Bible reveal a significant truth about what we should learn from people who made foolish decisions and the importance of what we can learn from God.

On the other side of the coin, when pride is an issue, false humility can be a deceptive tool the enemy uses. One of the aspects of being humble is that most people take it out of context. When God tells us to be humble (Micah

6:8) and how He opposes the proud, but gives grace to the humble, people take that to the extreme. They think that to be humble, they have to walk with their heads hanging down and speaking words that don't build or edify themselves. For instance, people who feel like they are living a godly life by being humble will say "Oh, I could never do that!" However, this is not how God instructs us. Being truly humble the way God tells us is to speak the promises of His word and declare that "we can do all things through Christ who strengthens us"(Phil 4:13). True humility is seeing how valuable we are, being grateful of the gifts God has given us, and knowing that there are many things we can accomplish as long as we see Him as our source of strength. As we seek the wisdom of God simply by asking Him for wisdom, we start to realize how to benefit from His word and how to put His teachings into proper context. Another instance where I encountered many Christians who take humility out of context is when someone comes to them to say a big "thank-you." They will not accept any thanks, but tell that person to say thank-you to God. In one sense that is good, but we still need to give thanks to one another, as God instructs us to. He tells us to give credit to one to another when credit is due. Receiving thanks from one to another is not the problem, it becomes a problem when we handle praises from others to have the attitude that says "look at what I have done." Receiving thanks should be done, but with a humble heart and having an attitude of gratitude. People who never graciously accept any thanks, live in a false humility concept, because we need people to show gratitude to one to another by being thankful to one another. People who take God's word to the extreme need to know how to accept thanks without feeling guilty about it while being able to guard against becoming proud. These are amongst many things of how people take the word out of context and don't know how to apply the wisdom of His word to their lives in order that they may benefit fully. The difference of becoming proud and being humble is that two people can say the exact same thing, and declaring that "I can do this." But the proud man would not even acknowledge God, while the other one would be speaking positive words that are based on what God says, and acknowledge his or her need for God. The wonderful promises of God are reserved for us to declare because if God says them, then, it is obviously His will for us in the first place. This reminds us that we need to keep our focus on how God observes us and sustains us. When we have true humility, we come to know the truth that without God, we can do nothing (John 15:5b), but also knowing that we can accomplish much when we realize our dependency of Him. Knowing the truth about humility and what God teaches us, is one of the paramount structures of our lives that God is able to establish in us. Otherwise, when we fail to be humble, we fall just like Nebuchadnezzar did, and our lives, whom we should be building upon, ends up coming down with great destruction (Prov 16:18).

You will often notice that many television commercials advertise products that help make women look more beautiful with creams, lotions, make-up which may be very good at maintaining their physical youth. While at the same time, as they put emphasis on the outward appearance, they fail to care for their inward being. When I meet many different people, I find that real beauty always comes from within, by having a pure heart. I like what God tells us in Ecclesiastes 8:1(b) "that wisdom brightens a mans countenance and changes its hard appearance." In fact, what makes the person is their inner man. The flesh in which we live in, is simply an outer shell of our real person. When we leave this world, our physical bodies are left behind in the grave and our inner soul and spirit being is what lives in the eternal realm. Therefore, it is vital that we care for who we really are by preserving our inner being. This comes by exercising our minds to become healthy, just as God instructs us. In Phil 4:8, Jesus tells us to think on things that are lovely, pure, holy, good because He knows that the mind is a powerful attribute we have and when we don't use it to benefit our well being, we become destructive in our behavior towards ourselves and others. People who live their lives as criminals and a lifestyle that is totally ungodly, first started by not giving careful heed to their thoughts and not being mindful of how to think thoughts that would otherwise edify oneself. What we watch, is a gateway to the mind which often causes us to justify our destructive behavior. In Matthew 6:22,23, you will read that the eye is an entry that makes our whole body either light or being full of darkness, then how great is that darkness. That is why pornography is so destructive because when people entertain these sights to enter the mind, it causes people to do the most hideous crimes. It all started just looking through with the eyes. If these people had not used their eyes to look at these sights, they would not have ended up doing the unthinkable. After David had committed adultery with Bathsheba, he understood later why he committed this act when he looked and lusted after her. This is why he confessed by making a covenant with his eyes so he would not sin with them. This goes right to the very beginning when satan tempted Eve to eat the forbidden fruit, which the devil had her look at, which caused her to lust and forget what God had instructed so clearly moments before this incident occurred. This is another aspect of how subtle sin is and how it blinds people from coming to know the truth about God and our purpose in life.

There is a wonderful book that has been written by a highly regarded psychologist, who is a Christian. A book titled "who switched off my brain" written by Dr Carolyn Leaf. She tells us scientifically that proves God's word that our mind can in fact be corrupted just by the way we think, and how the physical anatomy of the brain is in fact deteriorated from thinking negatively about ourselves and when we focus on any negative circumstances and from listening to words that have been destructive. No wonder God says in Philippians 4:18 that He admonishes us to let our minds dwell on whatever is honorable, whatever is right, whatever is pure, whatever is lovely, whatever is of good repute, if there is any excellence or worthy of praise, to think upon these things. He knows above anyone else that our souls become healthy or unhealthy just by the way we think upon. I was really intrigued of how Dr Leaf proves with scientific theory that just thinking and speaking negatively does real damage to the brain, while at the same time, thinking healthy thoughts and speaking God's encouraging word over our situation helps restore the brain tissues. This is why I cannot say enough about how vitally important it is to have a desire to gain not only knowledge of God's word, but also an understanding about Him and His word. The neat thing about God and how He is able to bless the minds of people is that He Himself imparts knowledge, wisdom, understanding and insight to those who desire this, by asking, believing and receiving what He is able to do. Just as a person like Mary had often pondered His word in her heart, this is when we are blessed with the wisdom and knowledge of His word. In Proverbs 14:6(b), God tells us that "knowledge comes easily to the discerning". I can truly testify to this. As I often just sit silent and meditate and give thought of what I read in the Bible, it is often at that time which God reveals a deeper knowledge and understanding of a concept.

Another wonderful truth I have come to know was after I had been a victim for several years, by dwelling on negative words spoken against me, to the point of wanting to quit living and just wanting God to end my life. After I have heard and received revelation of God's message about our thoughts and how we can overcome being a victim with the power of His word, I decided to exercise my right as a child of God to speak the authority of His word to encourage me and deliver me from the destruction of negative words spoken against me. Over a period of time, by speaking the encouragement of God's word over my situation, I have never felt better about myself than I ever have. It is a real testimony that I am alive today to tell you that God's word works and is positive if we first of all believe what He say about us and we accept His encouraging word for ourselves.

Another destructive agenda is that many people will consider lust and other such minor actions to be a "little" sin and they will brush it off as though it doesn't mean much. However, we need to remember that sin is what cost Christ to come to this world and live an agonizing life of sorrows. Not only was He rejected by His disciples, He also went through agony in the garden of Gethsemene until finally, it cost Him the shedding of His Blood and dying on our behalf. This is the reason why it is important to remind ourselves to focus on Jesus and the penalty on the cross He bore for us due to the sin of mankind through Adam.

What is very helpful is when we make a list of what we are to be thankful for. We can effectively remember how blessed we often are, which would otherwise have been forgotten and may have given way to a complaining spirit or ending up being defiled, which stems from having a root of bitterness. Failing to remember how blessed we really are, is a sign that often causes Christians to stumble and become thankless. The most effective way I remember is to keep a diary or a "book of remembrance" on what God has done for us in so many ways. Even the smallest agenda where we think is insignificant can be a great reminder to us that He cares enough for us for even the smallest matters. One of the other reasons that Christians don't preserve their relationship with God by keeping spiritually healthy is because they often take everything for granted. We fail to understand the truth of how blessed we really are when we can go to our kitchen tap and open the faucet to enjoy clean drinking water. When we can live with a roof over our heads, sleep on a nice comfortable bed, drive our vehicles and enjoy many other small amenities during the course of the day, we are better off than over two thirds of this world's population. Many people of Africa and other third world nations often have to walk many miles with a bucket to obtain clean water, if any. Some as young as small children are often left for this arduous task, where they never learned to have fun compared to the activities kids take for granted in the more affluent countries. We end up thinking this is our right and by our standards, we have been the reason for our own good fortune. Again, the story of Nebuchadnezzar should be a reminder of how grateful we need to be to God for providing everything we enjoy in life, when sadly, we often take for granted. Unfortunately, he had to eat and live like a wild ox long enough for his nails to grow like claws before he came to his senses (Dan 4:33,34). One of the stumbling blocks that cause people to turn away from God is when they question God critically, "why do so many people suffer?" When those of us who do not suffer like the rest, we should remember that we are to be thankful. This should be a reminder for us to truly be thankful when we see others far less fortunate. Unfortunately, when many of us consider the "haves," we often continue to be totally thankless, even though we see others with next to nothing. Failing to remember the goodness of God and how He takes care of us causes pride to enter. As indicated in the previous chapter, pride is a spirit that causes people who are either great or small to fall because pride is what blinds people of knowing the truth of their dependency upon God, whether they admit to it or not.

Today, many people identify humans are more blessed than others simply because they have more material wealth and are "more successful" by climbing the corporate ladder of success. We need to realize that though these may be a blessing, they often have a hidden curse, which is what causes many to fall by becoming proud. The way we need to visualize whether the material and monetary wealth is a blessing or a curse is to identify the character these bring about in us. If our character is polluted by becoming arrogant, prideful, or having a competitive, critical, judgmental spirit, what has intended to be a blessing may very well be a curse. When we keep our focus on eternal values and storing up rewards for us in heaven, God is not going to be interested in how much goods we acquired or how successful we climbed the corporate ladder in business. He is going to inquire from each of us what type of character we have developed by the type of relationship we had with Him and with one another. If having all this material wealth does not bring out the Godly character of having peace, joy, kindness, gladness, gentleness, temperance, goodness that develops deep rich relationship, then we are simply deceiving ourselves and we have lost our focus on what is important. Sadly, there are so many people in this world that are looking at acquiring material wealth to satisfy them, while they jeopardize their relationship with God and close knit friendships with others. At the same time, they become miserable and dissatisfied with life in general. The parable found in Luke 12:16-21 tells us about a rich man who was consumed about building his barns and acquiring his richness towards material gain rather than having a rich relationship with God. Jesus says about him "You fool, your soul will require of you this night". The result of this man's destruction was that he was not rich in his relationship to the Lord all because he was rich with the cares of this life of accumulating and focusing his richness to live the life of ease and being merry.

As I mentioned at the beginning of this book, I cannot emphasize enough to keep our focus on our relationship with God, and with one another to develop a Godly character which is the only way that gives us true peace, gladness and joy within that no material wealth could ever do. Keeping our focus on what God instructs us is how we live with purpose, the most blessed life. Compared to eternity, we have such an extremely short life span on earth. Even though we may live to be over 100 years, it is puny compared to eternity and it's like comparing a small puff of breath to a massive hurricane. How we live here on earth, either by following God's plan for our lives or by rejecting His authority is going to determine how we exist in all eternity, whether it be favorable, or unfavorable by being eternally condemned, which Christ often warned the Pharisees, Saducees and teachers of the law about. Having this mindset and focus has never been more important than now. The increase of technology has taken over many peoples lives, where it is meant to be a blessing, this is often what has brought a curse. Technology can be useful to our benefit to build us up depending on what we see and use, without becoming consumed with them. Sadly, to many people, television, Nintendo games, countless toys and other many such gadgets have brought dissention, division and separation into families. When families should be brought together, these many comforts in life we take for granted are the very things that have brought more destruction between family members which resulted in separating loved ones. As you may or may not have heard, a 15 year old teenager was obsessed by one of these electronic gadgets so much, that he lost the value of spending very little time with his parents and siblings. He failed to see the value of family unity, which can never be brought back from the past. This caused so much division between him and his parents, that he ran away from home, which sadly, was the last time he would ever see his own parents and siblings. Even while our elderly parents or grand-parents are still alive, it is invaluable that we build and maintain relationships while they are still living. All too often, loved ones die and the remaining family member's who haven't taken the time to spend quality time with them live in regret, because of the important things in life that is forever lost. The same thing holds true when we fail to choose the way which Christ lovingly tells us to go, we end up living in regret when we see the opportunities forever gone. When we focus on the purpose of our existence by living for God's glory (Isaiah 43:7) by allowing Him to be Lord of our lives and live by His wise counsel and instructions, God is able to preserve our lives with passion, purpose to which He paid the price in order that we can live the abundant life He offers us.

When we lose our opportunity to have our lives enriched by God, we do so by failing to remember the mercies God often gave us, which is another destructive spirit that causes many to stumble and robs many people from living the blessed life. God's mercies is Him relenting from destroying us when we otherwise deserved it. In Joel 2:13, God tells us in the latter part of the verse that He is gracious and compassionate, slow to anger and abounding in love, and He relents from sending calamity. When we have suffered injustice and the offender comes to us and asks us for forgiveness, many Christians sadly do not accept forgiveness. These are the people who forget how God shows mercy when they pleaded with God to forgive them. They are the only ones who have been robbed of the blessings that God wants to impart. Having unforgiveness is but feeding a selfish spirit within us that is anything other than God honoring. That is why God instructs us when we do not forgive others, God will not forgive us. It is not going to matter what circumstances occurred. We will never be justified harboring any unforgiveness no matter what. Our thoughts and attitudes have the power to build and preserve our lives or it can alter our lives and bring destruction that will adversely affect our eternal inheritance. In Matthew

18:23-35, Jesus tells a parable about how a servant was pardoned for an enormous amount of debt which he owed. He begged and pleaded for his patience to repay the master back. But the master (who we see as God) had compassion on this servant and forgave his enormous debt. Then this same servant went out and another one owed him a fraction of what he initially owed the Master. He would not even show any mercy or pardon of the tiny fraction of the price of what he had been pardoned. Later, the Master found out about how unmerciful this servant was and bound him chains and punished him severely. This is an indication of what happens to anyone who does not forgive others when God has immeasurably forgiven us, which is His warning of how He will deal with those who treacherously don't show mercy or forgiveness, when God Himself was exceedingly forgiving and merciful. This is why I cannot emphasize enough to forgive one another and be mindful of how much God has forgiven you. When we are not mindful of this, many people will forsake their faith whom God warns us in 1 Tim 4:1.

Another issue to learn about preserving our lives in order to remain healthy in all aspects, we need to train our tongues to speak blessings upon our lives and other peoples lives. It seems ironic that the smallest vessel in our bodies should be one of the most difficult members to control and manage. I can personally attest to that. James, a servant of Christ says in his book in James 3:5, 6 tells us how small our tongues are, but can corrupt the whole person and itself, set on fire by hell. When we consider this awesome power of the tongue, we need to pray for God's grace to help us bridle out tongue. In Proverbs 18:21, God tells us that death and life are in the power of the tongue. I have often proven this theory to be true. In one of many instances, a prominent singer from the past had taken her life from becoming anorexic simply because someone told her she was too fat. The destructive words spoken had truly taken its toll and life of an innocent victim that should never have occurred. There are probably thousands of others in the same way. People who have become a victim of bullying in schools have been known to take their own life. People who don't realize the consequences of their actions may have hindered hundreds of other lives to be touched by this person had he/she lived. The blessings that these victims could have helped will never be known. This tragic outcome happens when people do not understand the value of a human soul and the immeasurable accountability they unknowingly may have to give to God.

Acquaintances I have known throughout the years are simply a product of what they speak into their lives. A particular person I know of is a constant complainer who never has much positive words to say. Needless to say, this person has been through four marriages and continually lives under a curse of negative circumstances. For myself, for many years, I have spoken negative situations into my life which I have been a product of just that. Many times, people perish because of negative and poisonous words spoken towards us by others by their accusations. We don't have any control over the actions of others, but we can have control how those negative words affect us or not. Having indicated this in the previous chapter, I think it is worth repeating this paragraph, because of the seriousness of nature of how destructive our actions and words can be. Many times, I have experienced negative circumstances in my life because of what was adversely spoken against me enough times that

I began to believe what they said about me, of which I was a victim. After coming to the knowledge of God and seeking His word and His will for me, I realized that without the knowledge of God's word, I have been living in deception of believing the lies of people who speak negatively. When we see the power of God's word and the promises of what our Creator offers us, I decided to speak the Word of God over me and the abundant promises He mentions towards us. Even though we may do stupid things, God's mercy endures forever and pardons our iniquities when we repent. When I see the power of God's word defeat the devil, I decided to speak that same powerful word over my life over and over until I only believed what God said about me and refused to listen to the lies of human lips who opposed what God Himself said. I can tell you that it has profoundly altered my life and is truly life changing. I went from barely surviving each day to living a life with passion and purpose. But without this knowledge of the power and truth of God's word for us, He tells us in Hosea 4:6 that My people perish because they have rejected knowledge. Having the knowledge and understanding of scriptures while we exercise our authority which Christ has given us is the difference between living in victory or defeat. The scripture found in Luke 10:18-20 tells us that Christ has given His people authority over the spiritual enemy. Our victory in authority comes by speaking the word of God over our situation and saying the same thing God says and believing circumstances to come to pass. When you read 2 Tim 1:12, Paul declared that no matter what, that "for I know whom I have believed and am persuaded that He is able, to keep that which I have committed unto Him against that day." Knowing the truth about how much God's word is vital to us, we can expect to live life to the fullest while our very lives remain healthy and be preserved.

One of the ways that many people fall away from the faith is when they get so caught up with trivial matters and end up arguing over issues which really doesn't matter. I have seen at one time where a person was upset because someone else was sitting in the spot where they normally sit during a service, even though there were many other seats available. So instead of attempting to develop healthy relationships, which is what is really important, it ended up being jeopardized over such a trivial matter which should never have taken place to begin with. Often times, I see ourselves in many ways acting no better than the Pharisees and Sadducees. Noticed they were angry with Jesus who was doing a good deed by healing a man on the Sabbath day (Luke 6:6-11). They believed it was more important to keep the written law than to see the value of helping one another in their time of need. The ridiculous summary of this is that they felt justified trying to kill Jesus who they felt did not have any moral excuse of healing a human soul on a certain day of the week. This is absurd, but that is what sin does to a person when they forsake walking in the law of God, which is love. Being legalistic is often what blinds many Christians from understanding the principles of love because they focus their attention by keeping rules and regulations rather than the importance of demonstrating love, which is often violated because of it. For without love, anything we do for the Lord is totally meaningless (1 Corinthians 13:1-3). When we see the way the Pharisees and Sadducees acted, we may say to ourselves that this is totally ridiculous. But really, it often tells us how we can be similar in behavior in many other ways. I used to go to a church where people would look down on others simply because they weren't wearing a suit, or weren't dressed up according to their standards. The people who weren't dressed up to "their standard" ended up feeling inadequate when all times, we are commanded to love. Sadly, because of the actions of those who should have demonstrated love instead of judging wrongfully, this can very well be the pivotal point that can alter the lives of this particular family, to their benefit or destruction, simply because we either shared a warm smile or gave them the cold shoulder. Can you imagine Jesus standing at the door of the building where people were going to come and worship Him, and He would turn them away because they weren't dressed to a certain standard? This is the example I just mentioned about what it means to be legalistic. We need to see how vital it is to show love and compassion to others, because we should be focused on souls. Just think of that awful price it cost Jesus that He should have such great compassion, that when we were yet sinners (compared to a tattered garment) and being condemned, He gave His life for us.

One of the situations that is so grievous is when people within the church wrongfully judge others and slander one another because of a lack of understanding. As an example and without going into any details, a person was slandered by another brother in the church for accusing him of doing something despicable when all along, this person who was accused, wanted to join them in prayer because of his compassion. Instead of what was meant to be a good and honorable deed, was mis-communicated to another, which caused strife and division. In this case, an honest mistake that could have easily been forgiven and mended, ended up in hatred by the accuser. If the accuser would have known the heart of this individual, he would have dealt with the situation quite differently. The difference would have been unity, love and forgiveness. Because the accuser did not deal with the situation as Jesus instructs us, strife, factions and division became the result, which allowed the enemy to be active in his life. I would rather promote peace and restore relationships that build, edify and unite rather than causing strife and division which only ruins and destroys one another and has often destroyed the entire church, just because of a misunderstanding. Just think of the difference a family can be when comparing a family in turmoil to one that is unified in love, peace, understanding and harmony simply because they understand the factor of true love, pursuing peace and maintaining unity. What a tragedy this will be when every accuser realizes he has been deceived by the real enemy who is out to destroy humanity in the first place. I can truly believe that every accuser is deceived because there will never be a time when we have to give an account before God, that anyone will ever be justified by being angry and harboring an unforgiving spirit towards another. The unfortunate aspect of this scenario is that the accuser had believed a lie about this other gentleman. If he had known the underlying truth about his heart, they would have been best friends instead.

Another tragedy about situations like this is when those who accuse end up spreading venomous words that spread through gossip and slander. The worst thing about it is when people who listen to gossip don't put a stop to it. This is one of the things that Christ reminds us about maintaining justice. Again, when it comes right down to it, we will have to give an account on how we treated one another. This is why I can't emphasize enough to be focused on becoming "Peace makers" and realize that how we treat others is exactly how we treat the living God. That is why Christ tells us not to let the sun go down in our anger otherwise, we give the devil a foothold in our lives and give him access (Ephesians 4:26), just like when satan entered into Judas Iscariot who betrayed Jesus and ended up hanging himself in remorse. In the beatitudes, Christ tells us that we are blessed when we are peacemakers. This is what should make us different from the world. Jesus mentions in (Matt 5:46,47), that if you only love those who are lovely, do not the pagans do the same? If you only greet those you only associate with, how different are you from the world? We need to show the world what it means to be a Christian, whereby true genuine love is shown to each one. No one will ever be justified by gossip, slander, back-biting each other, no matter what has taken place. When they stand before Christ, He is not going to see if they are justified by what they did which God clearly tells us to refrain from doing, but He will ask them "Why did they not choose to pray for that person instead?" Because this is what God admonishes us to do. God tells us when gossip and slander cease, the fire ceases to spread its destruction, "without wood a fire goes out; without gossip a quarrel dies down" (Proverbs 26:20). To know that this device is one of satan's destruction, we should have the wisdom to do what our loving God instructs us to do. God Himself always admonishes us to choose His ways which leads to peace. Denying the leading of His Spirit of Wisdom, is the result of receiving anything other than peace and reaping the consequences of our destructive actions.

Another reason why anger is easily stirred up in people is because they think other people, family members, coworkers, acquaintances, including the spiritual leaders or people in full time ministry are here to serve them and continually feed them. The problem is that people focus on their own needs rather than on what they could be doing for others. This is what fills people with peace and gladness: is because they seek to be a blessing to one another. The Apostle Paul tells us in Hebrews 3:13 to encourage each other daily so that we would not be hardened by sins deceitfulness. We were made in the image of God to be a blessing to one another, just as God delights to do for those who love Him. That is why it is more blessed to give than to receive (Acts 20:35). When we are more concerned with serving self, God tells us that we cannot serve Him at the same time. If what we have gives God the glory, we can never go wrong, when what we have seeks to glorify self, then we are not in right standing with God. For Jesus tells us in John 7:18 "He who speaks on his own does so to gain honor for himself, but he who works for the honor of the one who sent him is a man of truth, there is nothing false about him." Therefore, God is most pleased when we live to give Him glory by serving others rather than seeking to serve self at the expense of others.

When we lose our focus on the importance of love, Jesus reminds those who were upholding the law that they should have been focused on what really matters to God; maintaining justice, showing mercy and remaining faithful (Matthew 23:23,24). Jesus was harsh towards the teachers of the law, when He retorted to them about being hypocrites and blind gnats, because they thought they were more justified by keeping rules and regulations. Therefore, it is so vital to ensure that our motive is always done in love and being merciful. It is important to know that how we treat others is exactly how we treat the Lord. Jesus was indicating to His disciples in (Matthew 25:37-40), that when He was sick, or in prison, they visited Him there. When He was hungry and naked, they fed and clothed Him. The disciples asked Him, Lord when did we see you sick or in prison? When were you naked or hungry? His reply is that when we have done it unto others, we have done it unto the Lord. If a lot of Christians treat the Lord like they treat the least of the brethren, they would be showing contempt towards Jesus.

The Bible also tells us that we are to have balance in life. In Proverbs 20:10, He mentions about how He hates differing weights. This is when people will go to the extreme on several issues. As an example, people who become Christians can be so heavenly minded that they are no earthly good, which means that they will entirely disassociate themselves from sinners and forsake to reach out to others in their time of need, who need to know Christ in the first place. I like what Jesus tells His disciples, that the sick are the ones who need a doctor, not those who are well. He Himself had often associated with sinners. The Pharisees and Sadducees often mocked Him because He ate along with the sinners and tax collectors. How else could He minister to those if He disassociated Himself from them in the first place? All too often, this is the mentality of many Christians who need to be a light for Christ to those who are in need.

When Jesus was telling about maintaining justice, I believe He was talking about being there for those less fortunate, such as the widow and the fatherless as He tells us in (James 1:27). When we show mercy, we need to remember that if God was not merciful to us, we would all be condemned. When we fail to show mercy, it is because we have forgotten that God is always merciful to us. By being merciful, we are to look past the faults of others and see their needs. We never will know what background our oppressors may have endured as a child. I can tell you that the experience I often face, when I ask the Lord to forgive me, I often will have the strength to specifically pray for my enemies as Christ taught us to do. It's at that time when we are seeking God's mercy for us, that we are able to offer mercy unto others. Especially when a lot of people who choose to live apart from allowing God to build their lives, may never consider to forgive others when they trespassed or offended them. Therefore, in order that we may continually be built up in the Lord, it is important to remember how often God has been merciful to us, we can then be free from harboring bitterness which defiles many and have the ability to show mercy instead. When we fail to show mercy and do otherwise, we end up being robbed of living the blessed life which Jesus had suffered on our behalf, and we are the only ones who suffer loss. We end up losing our peace and joy in this present life and lose much of our eternal rewards just because we followed our fickle emotions simply because we didn't feel like showing mercy or we justified not showing mercy to one another. No one is going to be responsible for our actions, nor are we going to be responsible for anyone's actions, no matter if we are directly or indirectly involved. Although others may have wronged us, we are going to be responsible of how we reacted to any given situation, whether favorable by following God's direction or unfavorable by rejecting His instructions for us.

One of the major issues in my life that was likely a hindrance from my growth is when a person is jealous and becomes competitive. The root of being jealous and competitive stems from feeling insecure about yourself. When a person feels insecure, they have a tendency of becoming a perfectionist, become competitive and if you examine others and perhaps yourself, these type are the ones who become unhappy because others are succeeding and they feel like they are not. When feeling insecure, they don't see themselves measuring up to the worlds standards of what others expect of them. When I saw myself like that, I felt I had to go the extra mile to fight being insecure and I saw how competitive I became. I would feel better about myself when I did better than others after examinations from High school or college and compared to where I stood in ranking in a classroom. Having this type of spirit within me was destroying my life. I was being eaten away because when it comes right down to it, we are always seeking the approval of others when we put ourselves in this situation. What has helped me over the years is when I became a believer and decided to allow God to build my life, I used the principles of what I talked about in the earlier chapters by meditating of how God showed His love for me through His Son Jesus by living the humble life He chose to do and be lead through many valleys, agonized in Gethsemene, was mocked, chastised and died the most agonizing death on the cross. I had to personalize what He says about His life, which He offers me. Also, when I chose to believe who I am because of what He says, I am uplifted. God tells me that I am the apple of His eye, that He loves me with an everlasting love, that He gives us the right to be Children of God to those who believe. That means that whatever He has, we can enjoy because we are His children. Just as a young child growing up in a family, has all that is available which belongs to his/her parents, so it is the same to those of us who believe in His name. This is something that each of us need to speak to our spirit and insert our names to tell us how much God loves us. I now realize more and more that whatever the Bible says about us, it is absolute and anything else spoken about us otherwise is nothing but a lie. I also had to change my thinking to believe and know that God accepts me, even though much of the world may not. When you know God accepts you, nothing else is going to matter what other people think of you. Even though you could do the nicest things for others, they may still never accept you. The life of Jesus is the best classic example of how He loved the world, yet much of the world hates and rejects Him. The question is why? Because, people don't bother to take the time they need to, in order to find out about who God is and what He should mean to them. Just like Paul tells us in Phil 3:10, that He was determined to know Jesus and allow the power of His resurrection to be able to flow into his life. It wasn't even enough for Paul to know about Him, but it was vitally important to this Apostle to know Jesus personally.

Having an insecure spirit that was the cause of harboring jealousy and bitterness was a serious bondage I knew God had to deal with me, which I can now say that He has liberated me from. When we take the time to do an inventory of how we see ourselves and to be honest with ourselves by confessing our faults to God, He wants to help us and bless us more by building and restoring our lives to what it should be in order to live the life to the fullest. Picture this scenario as someone living in a house which needs to be repaired and restored. If your anything like me, I can't even begin to think of where to start of how I can ever fix any part of a house. I have enough challenges building a small square box!! Therefore, if I see that the house which I live in needs repairing and restoration, I am going to call on someone I have a lot of respect for and trust to do the job properly. It will cost us financially to get this done, but the house will be restored. Our house is like our bodies, because God tells us that our bodies are His temple (1 Cor 6:19,20). Likewise, God wants us to call on Him to restore our very soul which He is most capable of doing, but like the carpenter, we need to call upon God. The thing what may cost us is not finances, but the cost of allowing God to do His work is by us doing our part by making changes to our agenda to spend more time with God, seeking His will for us by what the bible tells us and be determined to believe what He says who He is. It may cost us by changing the way we think and meditate on the truth about what He says about us. Feeling insecure is believing the lies of the devil and not understanding how much God loves you. This was a stronghold in my life which I can now say how liberating it is to no longer live like this when I allowed God to build me up and restore areas of my life that I knew which needed to be restored. Although some may say, where was God when I felt insecure? Now that I am liberated from this bondage by allowing Him to change my circumstance, I would never know how great it is to know how He is able to be a Restorer of my life if I have never needed this to be done in my life in the first place. This also reminds me how important it is to keep Him in our schedule as our high priority if we expect to allow our lives to be built and live with passion and purpose. This also reminds me that no matter how bad your past may have been, God can make any negative past experiences to be a blessing to many others that are in the same situation. Therefore, we can boldly claim the truth of His word that "And we know that all things work together for good for those who love the Lord and are called according to His purpose (Romans 8:28)." We can see how powerful His word is when we experienced circumstances in our lives and allow Him to build and restore our lives. Therefore, the bible is not just a bunch of philosophical phrases that just try to make us feel good about ourselves, but it is a powerful truth if we will appropriate His promises for ourselves. God tells us, "For the message of the Cross is foolishness for those who are perishing, but to us who are being saved, it is the power of God (1 Cor:18).

Some instances which may cause people to withdraw is because they feel they don't measure up to God's expectations. They believe the false concept that if they accomplish many tasks, then they will be justified. This is nothing but a lie, because God tells us several times in scripture that our works is to simply believe in the One whom the Father has sent, which is believing in Jesus. In James 2:23, it indicates that Abraham was justified simply because He believed in what God told him. It didn't say anything about being justified for what he ever did. In 1 John 5:5, God asks the question: "Who is it that overcomes the world? Only he who believes that Jesus is the Son of God." It's encouraging to know that we are in right standing with God simply because we believe who God says about Jesus and believes what the word says, for Jesus is the fulfillment of the word (John 1:1,14). That doesn't mean we can't be used to do good works, but we need to remember that we aren't justified by good works (Ephesians 2:8,9). God mentions about being pure, just by simply believing that we have the hope of becoming like Christ, not ever attaining it by our good works (read 1 John 3:2,3). When people don't believe they can be used of God, I can testify that this is a lie. God created man to give Him glory (Isaiah 43:7). Therefore, if He created each one of us to give Him glory, then we have the ability to do so. God created each one of us to do a special and unique work that no one else can do. I can testify that when I was a young adult, just having left home, I truly believed that I was created by accident and I had no value to give. I sincerely believed and questioned why I was created because I felt I was of no use to anyone. After I have received Jesus to come in and be Lord of my life, I am continually amazed of what God is able to do through me that I could never have imagined. If someone were to tell me that I would have accomplished so much in life so far, I would have told them to quit dreaming. This has nothing to do with my own ability, but is a testimony of what God is able to do through anyone who will simply believe and see what God is able to do through you when you desire to be a blessing to others and to be able to give Him glory. This is why I want to really emphasize of what a tremendous builder He can be to each of us. The reason why God doesn't work through a lot of people is because they simply do not believe. In Matt 13:58, Jesus could not do many miracles in his own hometown because people did not believe. Unbelief is a horrible deterrent that literally stops the blessings of God to flow through us and we lose more than we can imagine on earth and the rewards we could have received just because we chose not to believe. People may lose their homes through disasters, lose their investments because of a financial crisis or corruption. But these unfortunate incidents will never compare to the loss people forfeit their eternal inheritance just because they chose not to believe in Jesus, or believe who they are in Christ after they have received Him into their lives, or not believe what God is able to do for them. The cost of choosing not to believe is astronomical.

Sometimes, when people fall away from the faith which God has initially built up in their lives, they end up failing to discern the words spoken that may be false teachings. When people don't take the time to study the bible and search what is spoken to them about an issue or any doctrine, they start to believe others rather than what Jesus taught. As a couple of examples of many, there are ministers in different mainstream religions who now preach that Jesus is not the actual Son of God, nor do they believe in the resurrection of Jesus. Sadly, many people have listened to these false teachings and have been blinded from the truth. This is where Jesus mentions about the blind leading the blind. In 1 Corinthians 15:17, Paul plainly tells us that when we don't believe in the resurrection, we are still in sin no matter what, and our faith is entirely futile. In verse 34, he tells us to come back to our senses because they are ignorant of God and says this to their shame. No matter how many good works we do and what we accomplish in life, if we come to believe a lie such as this, we will never be justified no matter what. A nationally recognized Bishop even preaches that there is no resurrection, even though the Bible is quite clear on this issue. People who end up believing there is no resurrection have lost the pivotal purpose of what the Christian faith is all about. For if there is no resurrection, what good is believing the remaining portion of the Bible? Another primary concern about listening to false teachings is that there are many professed Christians who believe in the theory of evolution rather than believing they were wonderfully and fearfully created by an awesome intelligent designer of our bodies, whereby only God could create. God Himself could not be any clearer about the fact that He created man in His own image. I would far rather know that I am created in His image than any other form, and only be designed by no one other than God than to think that I would have just evolved from a lineage of apes or created by accident from a blob of cells. When we fail to give heed to what is being said and line up to what God says, we become lazy and desensitized and end up believing doctrines which God Himself clearly opposes. The Bible is in fact the inspired word of God and He tells us that He created man. I can truly say that what God says about creation is much more encouraging than what man says. Whenever someone man would bring discouragement to me, I would go to God and read His word and believe what He says about me and I am uplifted with His encouraging word. By making His word the authority in my life, I have lived a much more peaceful, purposeful and fulfilling life than I ever have in the past. These are just some of the many doctrines that false preachers are preaching to anyone who will simply listen to them and not bother to check it out in the Bible. In 2 John 7-11, God warns His people about many deceivers. Even in verse 11, He tells us that when we welcome these people into our homes who preach false doctrine, we share in their wickedness. This tells me that because our bodies are compared to a house and we are God's temple, we need to refuse to entertain any false teachings to enter into our hearts. In 1 Timothy 4:1-16,

Paul tells us in verse 16 that we need to watch our lives and doctrine closely. Persevere in them, because if we do, we will save both ourselves and our hearers. When we don't see the Bible that feeds the soul to be just as important as food feeding the body in order to stay alive, we end up not having the true value and importance of God's word which is the key to eternal life. When we compromise God's word and don't take time to compare what is being preached, its like stripping and severing a lifeline to our soul that eventually leads us to our eternal destiny. Peter replied back to Jesus after He asked His twelve disciples if they were going to leave Him like the many other disciples had. I think this is worth mentioning again, that Peter replies, "To whom shall we go? Only You have the words to eternal life." Peter is also saying that if we rely on any other word to be our authority, it will only lead down the path that leads other than to eternal life. When people believe what is said by false teachers and false prophets over what the Bible tells us, then how can they say that Jesus is their Lord if they don't use His word as their final authority? Jesus tells His disciples, "how can you call me Lord and not do the things I command you to do?" Otherwise, we ultimately fail to allow God, who is the greatest One to effectively build our lives with passion and purpose.

We need to watch by being faithful. This is where we need to have integrity by acting the same way behind closed doors as we would be if we had the Pastor over at our place. We would be the same on each day of the weekday calendar as we would be when we put on our Sunday best. Being faithful is doing what is right, even though we may never be rewarded from anyone else because of it. Building a healthy mindset, enriching our relationship with God by having healthy relationships with one another is what is really going to count in the end. In 1 Cor 1:9, God calls us to have fellowship with Jesus, who is faithful. This is what it means to allow God, who is the greatest One who is able to build us up, to fulfill and enrich our lives in every way during this period of our lives on this earth and life eternal. No wonder Jesus tells us that by living according to His commandments by loving Him and one another, we end up living the abundant life now and forever which He offers us. When we focus on God as a Just God, we will be strong in character because we will never be dismayed by unfavorable circumstances, but will always have that endless hope and peace knowing that our God is faithful.

Storing up eternal rewards that will last us for all eternity rather than any rich rewards that will simply last during our span of existence here on earth would be a most significant benefit. This doesn't mean we can't live for today in order that we forsake our joy and peace simply to just live for the future. After all, the type of life which Christ lived was a sacrificial life in order that we can live the abundant life each and every day. However, I'd far rather have the richness of His blessings that will last forever rather then to forsake eternal rewards just for a mere moment in time. The thing we need to remember is not to be so focused on living for the moment when it means that we forsake storing for ourselves treasures of rewards in the eternal realm which means to live in obedience to what the Bible tells us. One of the ways we forsake our eternal rewards is when we seek to be a people pleaser or simply focus to receive the honor and praises from each other in order to seek our own glory. Especially when we may be violating God's laws when it means simply to please man. In Matthew 6:1

and 2, Christ tells His Disciples that if they seek to receive the glory from others, they end up forsaking the rewards to which our Heavenly Father would have given. I can tell you that whatever God rewards man, it is far greater than receiving any autonomous reward from any man because when God Himself rewards, these are the rewards that will last forever, where no one else or any circumstance will ever be able to rob from us. Mans reward and the glory received will only last for a mere moment in time, then easily forgotten shortly thereafter.

The people of Jerusalem were strong because the Lord Almighty is their God (Zechariah 12:5), which means they followed the commandment of love by obeying Him. The Holy Spirit, which Jesus tells us He sent to do a precious work in us (John 16:13) is the Greatest Builder for our life if we are willing to allow Him to do that precious work in our lives. The Holy Spirit reveals to us the knowledge of what Jesus has accomplished for us. I am a living testimony that God is able to do a far greater work in me than I ever dreamed I could ever accomplish. Unless you are totally yielded to God, you will never know the power, wisdom, knowledge and ability, which He is able to build your life as His true ambassador (2 Cor 5:20).

Finally, If we expect to allow God to be the greatest builder of our lives, we need to be determined to believe what He says, no matter what is going on in our lives. God wants us to be strong in Him because when we are strong in Him, no unfavorable circumstances happening to us or around us will ever rob us of the peace, joy (steady calmness), and gladness. No wonder the Bible says in Neh 13:8 "the joy of the Lord is our strength." I can truly say when I made that decision to became bold (by being determined), decided to take a stand and not allow circumstances to rule my life and dared to believe no matter what, I became a testimony to tell you that I am no longer a victim of negative circumstances, but am now living the life of what Jesus intends for us to have "life in abundance, to the full till it overflows." Sometimes we need to be violent against the enemy who wants to rob, kill and destroy our lives, because when we are violent in the right way, God tells us in Matthew 11:12 "From the days of John the Baptist until now, the kingdom of God has been forcefully advancing, and forceful men lay hold of it." This means that we need to be purposeful to have a determined spirit and an attitude that says "we will not give up" and with the help of His Holy Spirit, being able to endure to the end. When we are lukewarm and have that apathetic and passive attitude, we become like an inactive individual that fails to exercise his body physically, which in a short period of time, he becomes unfit. We fail to be anything else but strong and encouraged as God tells us to be many times in His word. The reason why many have this attitude is because they never take the time to learn who Jesus really is and what He could mean to each of them. When we take the time to take an inventory of our attitude, whether good or unfavorable, it all comes down to how much time we have invested to spend time with God, read His word, talk to Him in prayer, listen to good tapes, watch TV programs that preach the encouraging and goodness of His Word and spend time with other believers in order to fellowship with, to be an encourager and be encouraged. We become what we feed our spirit. We need to value our time that is going to count each day that will give us eternal value and rewards. If we apply these principles to invite God to effectively build our lives, His Holy Spirit, who is able to be our Comforter, Helper, Healer, Restorer and Provider is in fact, the greatest Builder and Architect for our lives. The work of His Holy Spirit is only able to be as effective in our lives to the degree of how much we believe the truth of His word, believe that our outcome will be the very best when we commit our lives in His hands and willingly allow Him to work and build our lives most effectively.

Printed in the United States
144446LV00001B/3/P

9 781438 966458